THE DOCTOR IS NO LONGER IN

CONVERSATIONS WITH U.S. PHYSICIANS

Drs. MaryAnn Wilbur & Katherine Rieth

The Doctor is No Longer In: Conversations with U.S. Physicians

Copyright © 2024 Dr. MaryAnn Wilbur & Dr. Katherine Rieth.

All rights reserved. No part of this publication may be reproduced, distributed, or transmitted in any form or by any means, including photocopying, recording, or other electronic or mechanical methods, without the prior written permission of the publisher, except in the case of brief quotations embodied in critical reviews and certain other noncommercial uses permitted by copyright law. For permission requests, write to the publisher, addressed "Attention: Permissions Coordinator," at the address below.

ISBN: 979-8-9904015-1-8 (softcover)
ISBN: 979-8-9904015-0-1 (hardcover)
ISBN: 979-8-9904015-3-2 (eBook)
ISBN: 979-8-9904015-2-5 (audiobook)

Cover design thanks to Ms. Sofia Gonzalez, Affluence Media Agency. Interior design/formatting by Vickie Swisher, Studio 20|20.

First printing edition 2024.

MaryAnn Wilbur, MD, MPH, MHS
Director and CEO
Health Equity Consulting
15271 McGregor Blvd, Suite 16 PMB 415
Fort Myers, FL 33908

questions@thedoctorisnolongerin.com
mwilbur@healthequityconsulting.org

www.thedoctorisnolongerin.com
www.healthequityconsulting.org

DEDICATION

*This book is dedicated to our physician colleagues,
those who are still practicing
and those who have shifted their career paths.
Most importantly, we want to thank the physicians
who shared their stories in the making of this book.
We are honored by your courage and candor.*

AUTHORS' NOTES

This book began as a qualitative research project. We interviewed licensed physicians in the U.S.. We acknowledge that there are other important points of view and that some of the phenomena we describe are occurring globally. However, the goal of this particular project was to give voice to the U.S. physicians leaving direct patient care. These observations may not be generalizable to other populations.

Our participants were mostly recruited in person at a conference where physicians are seeking to learn about non-clinical career options. This audience overlapped strongly with our inclusion criteria and provided a wide demographic and geographic range. A few other participants were first person referrals. Trust was paramount to all involved. Through these introductions, we met over 100 colleagues wishing to participate who then filled out a short demographic survey. If a participant was willing, an interview was then scheduled. We continued interviews until reaching thematic saturation, consistent with Grounded Theory (Charmaz, 2014), which occurred at 35 interviews. We interviewed our physician colleagues and identified themes. Each chapter is a theme identified during the analysis. During the writing and the promotion of this book, we heard from over a thousand more colleagues and received valuable, and overwhelmingly affirmative, feedback.

We are incredibly grateful to our many colleagues who opened up and told us their difficult stories. For many physicians, being a doctor is an extraordinarily important part of their self-identity. For some, it is actually enmeshed with their identity to the point of impeding one's ability to recognize their own inherent worth separate from the role (Koretz, 2022). For everyone, though, to consider leaving this role is a desperate decision. For some, suicide seemed more rational. One participant told us that ***"to divorce my career was to divorce myself; is that even possible?"*** These interviews were often difficult to perform and to hear.

The physicians we interviewed told us about their fears, sorrow, and shame. To our colleague participants: we can't thank you enough for your courage and candor in sharing your stories of leaving direct patient care. And to those of our colleagues still caring for patients: thank you! We know your struggles, and we are all grateful for your determination. Our hope is that this project

Authors' Notes

will be just one small contribution to a larger movement in U.S. healthcare. Our system is broken. We need to understand the damage, learn from it, and create a system that works for everyone — from doctors to patients to communities.

CONTENTS

Dedication iii
Authors' Notes v

PART ONE

ORIGIN STORIES 1
Chapter 1: The Broken Spirit of the U.S. Physician 3
Chapter 2: How Did We Get Here? 13

PART TWO

THE SQUEEZE 25
Chapter 3: Loss of Control 31
Chapter 4: Burnout 43
Chapter 5: Dehumanization:
        Cogs Don't Have Needs 55
Chapter 6: Moral Injury 75
Chapter 7: Trust and Betrayal 91

PART THREE

THE PATH AHEAD 111
Chapter 8: Casualties and Consequences 113
Chapter 9: Where Are We Headed? 125

Notes 143
Acknowledgements 151

Part One

Origin
Stories

*"... at some point,
your spirit is broken,
and you can't find the strength
to fight anymore."*

— NEUROLOGIST AND FORMER DEPARTMENT CHAIR,
25 YEARS OF PRACTICE

CHAPTER 1

The Broken Spirit
of the U.S. Physician

At the behest of a mutual friend, the two of us scheduled a coffee date. "You are sharing the same reality right now," our friend said. "You two are practically the same person!" Our friend was right. We were two young(ish) female surgeons who were exhausted and disillusioned. We both have two sons, a puppy, and a complicated life outside of the overwhelm of working in today's healthcare system. We vented and bonded, and then we dreamed up this project.

We both love qualitative research. Unlike its quantitative brethren, qualitative research involves talking directly with individuals. It is about securing authentic stories and discovering themes; not computing numbers. We have both been performing this kind of research for years from both public health and anthropology backgrounds.

Over coffee, we shared our love for qualitative research. We also shared our frustrations and battle scars from years of clinical work. We both had many friends and colleagues "taking the leap" or "planning their escape" (the terms we have heard most people use in these situations, respectively). We knew just how bad our colleagues were hurting. We understood the desperation involved in walking away from something so closely intertwined with your identity. At the same time, we were following the media coverage on clinician burnout and the initiatives to tackle the problem.

As we watched huge efforts going into relatively superficial changes, we realized that the experts needed more information. They needed qualitative data. They needed authentic stories to understand that fixing electronic health records and improving reimbursement, although positive changes, would be insufficient to turn this around. We knew our own difficult stories. We both had friends who had left medicine, considered suicide, and sometimes both. We knew their troubling stories. And we knew that these stories needed to be told.

Retelling true stories is a powerful way to convey important information. There is a reason that we teach children complicated morals using fables, and we find cultures across the globe relaying ancestral information this way. Studies show that relaying information in this fashion cues separate parts of the brain and is much more likely to bring emotion into the experience, increasing the chances that the audience can understand, remember, and take action (Owen et al., 2021).

In the first interview for this project, we spoke to a Neurologist who had been practicing for well over 20 years. She had served as Department Chair and other important roles at her large institution. She told us how much she had previously enjoyed her career and was almost nostalgic about how things had been decades ago, during the years when she had been a junior faculty member and rising professor. But it all began to change around five years ago. New management came in, and there were drastic financial cuts. She was told when she would be working and how to practice medicine. Then, her nurse was fired without any discussion. These changes were experienced as both disruptive and disrespectful, and resulting problems escalated. When she spoke out, she was harassed and ultimately stepped down.

Our physician colleagues are suffering, all over the nation. There is good work being done to protect them from the immediate issues of suicide, addiction, divorce, and depression. The Clinician Burnout Foundation was established to assist with the immediate needs of burned-out physicians. SafeHaven was created specifically for clinicians who are suffering and in need of counseling. The Dr. Lorna Breen Foundation is a philanthropic effort to support such initiatives and was established in the name of a wonderful and accomplished physician who died by suicide.

There are also important initiatives trying to fix what has created this suffering: our healthcare system. Medicine Forward is a grassroots organization founded by physicians seeking to put the doctor / patient relationship back at the forefront of medicine. The International Conference Development (ICD) Healthcare Network is a curator of forums for best practices and has recently emphasized burnout management. New England Journal of Medicine (NEJM) Catalyst and similar venues consistently promote the content we will need to change the larger healthcare system. We will dive deeper into these conversations in the final chapters. First and foremost, however, this project is about giving voice to the doctors on the front lines.

During the writing of this book, Dr. Carrie Cunningham was the president of the Association of Academic Surgery (AAS). Dr. Cunningham is an extremely accomplished individual, surgeon, and leader. However, her success came at a price. In the years leading up to 2023, she had developed significant depression, anxiety, and alcohol dependence. In her outgoing presidential address, she courageously shared her personal story of mental health issues and the story of how she lost a close friend and colleague to suicide (Academic Surgical Congress & Cunningham, 2023). From one of her opening slides:

> ***Just because someone carries it well, doesn't mean it isn't heavy.***

Dr. Cunningham was quick to acknowledge that she had important protective factors on her side that likely explain why she is still here and some of our other colleagues are not. She reported extraordinary support from her family and friends. In a remarkable show of support from her institution, she continued to receive her salary while undergoing months of recovery and was able to keep her role and her title. This was strikingly different from the stories of the doctors that we interviewed. Dr. Cunningham finished her speech with the following statement and slide text below:

> ***Physicians need to practice in a space where this is a cultural norm:***
>
> ***We want you here.***
>
> ***We value you.***
>
> ***Your feelings are valid.***

Sadly, however, this is not the norm. Many of our colleagues have a story that starts out like Dr. Cunningham, but without the positive ending. Those are the colleagues that are leaving direct patient care. The goal of this book is to capture those stories. One might think getting at these stories would be easy, but physicians have been reluctant to share the details publicly. We knew that we would have to do this anonymously and with the same respect that we show other research participants.

So, we did just that. We spoke with our colleagues all over the nation, performing anonymous interviews. We then pooled these stories together and compiled them into this book. We made an intentional choice not to identify the physicians we interviewed. To maintain anonymity, we never tell one doctor's whole story. Every story told here is completely true, in that every experience shared was reported by one of our participants. However, to minimize the risk of identifying an individual participant, an anecdote may be an amalgamation of stories shared by two or three participants. This was done to minimize any finger pointing or downstream effects of this book on anyone, participants or otherwise. Every participant quote shared in quotations and in bold was transcribed verbatim.

All these physicians have impressive credentials. Quite a few of them have done such amazing things that to provide their credentials would be akin to using their names. Systemically discrediting physicians who are speaking up has become part of the problem and has allowed the situation to spiral to the point where we now find ourselves. We ask our readers to focus on the stories and the systemic issues, not on any individual. Our hope is that this book will spark important conversations and contribute to necessary changes in U.S. healthcare.

The physicians we interviewed are very different people. They represent different sexes, genders, and sexual orientations. They have varied history, ethnicity, and skin color. They represent most major medical specialties and every corner of the U.S.. Some of them work in large academic hospitals. Some of them are from small, rural private family practices. All of them either have left clinical medicine within the past two years or stated that they plan or hope to leave clinical medicine in the next two years. By "clinical medicine," we mean direct patient care. These doctors overwhelmingly told us that they love medicine, and they love their patients. However, they simply cannot continue providing direct patient care in the current environment.

We found a set of established and common experiences between the physicians we interviewed. The majority of these experiences are brought on by the current system of healthcare delivery and amplified by recent economic and social circumstances. Basically, these problems were here before, but COVID (and its sequelae) acted as a catalyst to make clinical medicine untenable.

This book has been a labor of love. We have thoroughly enjoyed the ridiculous, sad, devastating, and always authentic, stories our colleagues have entrusted to this shared goal. We are forever grateful for the trust they have placed in us. The experiences that they lived yesterday are currently being lived by a different physician today — one that maybe we can keep in our healthcare system to serve my mother or your son. As a society, we need to honor these stories, recognize our mistakes, and learn how to do better.

Our hope is that we connect with current physicians, upcoming physicians, physician leaders, healthcare administrators, patients, patient advocates, politicians, and anyone who has the power to shift how U.S. physicians experience their careers in the day-to-day. Ultimately, this is about improving the system as a whole — for those who are served (the patients, aka all of us) and those who are serving.

CHAPTER 2

How Did We Get Here?

As a group, physicians are a hardy bunch. Long hours, personal sacrifice, delayed gratification; these are all standard to a physician's existence. As a professional group, we have endured wars, epidemics, natural disasters, pandemics, and economic depression. We live up close and personal to the drama of human existence. We witness death, trauma, violence, cancer — and those things can happen to anyone. Add poverty to the mix and you see all of that, but with the indignity that society saves only for the poor.

Physicians have done this for centuries. Throughout American history, however, we have never seen a physician exodus like the one that is on the horizon. So, what is happening? Nothing substantial has changed about the physicians.

Nothing substantial has changed about the way we are educated or trained. Nothing substantial has changed about the patients. What changed? The context. The environment in which physicians work has changed. In the past 20 years, there was a major shift from physicians running a private practice to being employees of hospitals or medical systems. In 2012, approximately 20% of physicians were employed by hospitals. Just one decade later, in 2023, 80% were employed by hospitals. Small physician practices couldn't compete with large health systems (Darves, 2014; American Medical Association, 2023). Medicine had become a business.

The problem with this shift is that the business model of a large health system doesn't provide the environment physicians need to provide quality patient care. How did this happen? Below, we provide an absurdly simplified answer to this question. The following is an entire public health course distilled into a few pages. The goal is to give just enough background to understand the history, so we can get back to the matter at hand — assessing what is happening today and finding ways to renovate it.

A SYNOPSIS OF U.S. "HEALTH INSURANCE" AND "HEALTHCARE":

Prior to World War II, there was not an emphasis on accessing physician care among the general American population. With the advent of ether, antibiotics, quality imaging techniques and other notable discoveries, it became clear that accessing physicians and medical facilities would become important to the average American family, but it was going to be expensive for the common person.

With the onset of WWII, most of the men in our country went to war. Most of the women went to work in factories. Rosie the Riveter arrived on the scene. There was a federal cap on salaries, so that one factory could not steal a Rosie from one factory to another and slow production. Therefore, if an employer wanted to entice a particularly skilled Rosie, but could not challenge her salary, what could the employer offer to sweeten the deal? You guessed it: "health insurance."

The first company to market health insurance was Blue Cross Blue Shield. They offered employee-based "health insurance," more or less the way we know it today. However, the way that it was created is, in fact, illness insurance. It was intended to be used, "*if* you need healthcare." Nobody had experience thinking about health insurance, so it was set up much like flood insurance, home insurance, car insurance, or any other insurance.

For example, let's consider flood insurance. The insurance company takes a little money from every family and the family that experiences a flood gets what they need for repairs. It makes sense. Essentially, this is business people making calculated decisions. It's an educated gamble that not every family is going to experience a flood. What are the chances that *every* family is going to experience a flood? Not high. So, that gamble makes sense.

But if you take that logic to our health insurance, which is really illness insurance: what are the chances that *every* human body is going to break down? 100%.

The human body is mortal and will fail at some point. The chances that *every* person with coverage is going to need care is 100%. This means that the entire system was built with a fatal flaw. We have been trying to patch the system ever since. But each time we patch the system, we add burdens and obstacles and costs. We have done this so many times now, that we have arrived at a critical point. The patients are not being served. The physicians don't have what they need to serve the patients. Nobody is being served adequately by this system anymore. This is not going to work, and we are just about at the end of what this flawed system can provide.

We have seen this play out in multiple ways. We are the most expensive healthcare system in the world. We spend 18% of our gross domestic product (GDP) on health care (for comparison, the United Kingdom and Canada spend about 10% of their GDP on healthcare), yet we are the poorest in terms of outcomes of any developed nation — infant mortality, maternal mortality, life expectancy, among others (Papanicolas et al., 2018; Gunja et al., 2024). We have suffered in so many ways. Physicians are at higher risk for suicide compared to the general population (Rothenberger, 2017). We are experiencing a physician shortage that is getting more and more severe. In 2022, the American Medical Association (AMA) reported that 1 out of 5 physicians intended to leave direct patient care (Abbasi, 2022). The following year, the AMA reported that 40% of physicians are considering leaving their current practice (American Medical Association & Berg, 2023). This is happening. Sometime very soon, you are going to have to go to the emergency room for something, and there may not be a doctor to care for you (Shanafelt et al., 2021; Glatter, Papadakos, & Shah, 2023). We need to acknowledge that this has occurred because the system is fundamentally flawed.

The next step in understanding how we got here is to look at how our country took this flawed system of "health" insurance and made the insurance company the payer of medical bills, turning healthcare into a business.

A SYNOPSIS OF U.S. "HEALTHCARE" AS A BUSINESS:

In the U.S., the center of our healthcare system is not the patient; it is the dollar. We established illness insurance and then built an illness care system around it. The fee structure was then created based on "doing things." The doctor "does" something and bills for it. This is called a Fee-for-Service (FFS) system. It is basically the same way that you pay your mechanic. But we can probably agree that is not ideal. Don't we often worry about the mechanic doing unnecessary things to make money?

In addition, when the U.S. established this business, it did not implement the same regulations and antitrust laws that we have for other businesses. Not only did the government create healthcare to be a business, but it's a business that is ripe for short-sighted business practices that "squeeze" the source of income for the hospital system (e.g., the doctors). This structure allows for monopolization where big hospitals can engulf smaller ones without any consideration about the impact this may have on the local community.

We are seeing this across the U.S.. Have you noticed large hospitals acquiring smaller hospitals, turning into big conglomerates, and placing satellite locations under the same umbrella? That is good for business. If you are a business person and a monopoly is allowed, you are going to go for that. But that is not necessarily in the best interest of patient care. Some local hospital systems might be doing this to try to create a coordinated care system for the community they serve. However, there are many other systems that are simply seeking profit. When this happens, we see local maternity wards being closed, pediatric practices being moved from the neighborhoods they serve, and emergency rooms shutting down. This disrupts patient care, but it's being done in the name of business. And, not surprisingly, some communities are affected more heavily than others —

such that the people who are on the losing end of most things, are on the losing end *again*. For example, look at Black maternal mortality rates and the recent trends (Gunja et al., 2024).

To recap: we set up illness insurance, built an illness care system around it, and arranged fee-for-service (FFS) billing by the doctors. Those bills would then be paid by the insurance company, aka the "payer" (or payor). In the 1960s, the federal government established an insurance company for those people who are no longer working or who are unable to work: Medicare. Medicare drives reimbursement directly for many patients in the U.S. and indirectly establishes the normalized reimbursement rates for our private and employer-based insurance plans. The size, strength, and impact of Medicare has substantially driven change in reimbursement.

Our insurance companies were initially just the payers; they paid the bill. But Medicare implemented a big change that influenced how health insurance companies functioned. Medicare decided it wasn't going to just pay the amount that was being charged. It was going to negotiate the price down. This meant our third-party payers became discretionary negotiators. These negotiations created a gap between the cost of your surgery and what the hospital was paid for the costs of your surgery. And who pays the difference? You.

These changes took place, but with little to no transparency in the process. Despite efforts through the Affordable Care Act, such as the Hospital Price Transparency rule enacted in 2021, the process of what will be charged, what will be paid, and what you will owe remains largely opaque (Jiang et al., 2023). These changes also opened up a whole new way to siphon money out of this business model, because this gap became "business savings" for the insurance company. Not surprisingly, the employer-based insurance companies were happy to get on board. Once the siphoned money became standard profits for insurance companies, health insurance became recognized as big business.

In addition to these flaws, Medicare is also a regressive tax (meaning that it "hurts" the poor more than the rich, because what you have to put into the pot does not consider your wealth, or lack of). It is extremely expensive for most people. In the interest of curbing federal "spending," Medicare reimbursement has not been increasing at the same rate as the cost of delivering patient care. But it doesn't actually decrease the *cost* of patient care, it just decreases the reimbursement for the patient care. Our healthcare costs are still the same (or, more accurately, rising in the same way). This phenomenon of Medicare not keeping up with inflation has created a wider and wider gap. It has also led to medical debt becoming the number one cause of personal bankruptcy filings in the U.S. (Gottlieb, 2000; Himmelstein et al., 2019).

In summary, these are the main sources of our problem: (1) our insurance model, (2) our reimbursement model, (3) short-sighted business practices (including old-fashioned greed) and (4) poor regulation and lack of antitrust laws over U.S. healthcare as a business.

For the most part, we still have an FFS system, which inherently creates incentives for physicians to "do" more. This can increase healthcare costs. But it also feeds the perception that doctors do more than is needed. Regardless of whether you believe that or not, this perception opens the door for the business (insurance) to create obstacles between the doctor and the patient to maintain cost control. These obstacles usually fall under the heading of "utilization management" and result in increased cost. This is the push-back you get from your insurance company every time you want a new medication or want to schedule a procedure. The system keeps putting these obstacles in place as further checks and balances in an already broken system, until costs spiral out of control, and we land where we are today.

One of our research participants called it "administrative bloat." He felt like every time he approached his hospital administration about how to improve patient care, he was told there was not enough money. There was never enough money to make things better. He also said, ***"But, every time I turn around, there is another person being hired without a clinical background, whose job it is to tell me how to cut corners and how to do my job."***

Part Two

The Squeeze

"I've been buried alive, and I got out, and I will never allow that to happen again."

— PALLIATIVE CARE PHYSICIAN, 22 YEARS OF PRACTICE

"They've totally just ground me into dust."

— FAMILY MEDICINE PHYSICIAN, 20 YEARS OF PRACTICE

In this section, we will get to the heart of what physicians have been and are experiencing: loss of control, burnout, dehumanization, moral injury, and betrayal. These are the five themes that emerged from the interviews with our physician colleagues who are leaving direct patient care. These themes did not always fit into the categories already being discussed and described in current academic literature. We decided to let the themes emerge as they did (Charmaz, 2014). We believe these themes are generalizable to how our colleagues can be expected to report their experiences, if one were to repeat this process.

That being said, we understand that anytime you offer new information on a complicated subject, there is a desire to integrate this new information into an established body of knowledge. After the interviews were completed and we were writing this book, we had the opportunity to meet with several experts on these matters. We are deeply grateful to these individuals for their perspectives and feedback.

In these discussions with experts, we found that some components of well-known and extensively described phenomena, such as burnout and moral injury, were felt and described as separate experiences among many of our participants. By definition, clinician burnout is "a syndrome characterized by exhaustion, depersonalization and a sense of ineffectiveness related to one's work" (Shanafelt et al., 2002; Maslach & Leiter, 2016). This can manifest in different ways, such as the exhaustion of "do more with less," a feeling like you can never keep up or that your efforts make no difference. We see examples of this throughout Chapters 3, 4, and 5.

Similarly, moral injury has a strict, but encompassing, definition. "Moral injury is defined as perpetrating, failure to prevent, bearing witness to, or learning about acts that transgress deeply held moral beliefs and expectations" (Dean, et al, 2020).

Again, we appreciate how many different ways this might manifest from one individual to another, such as (1) frustrations with the inability to provide quality care and (2) feeling betrayed by your leadership. These two experiences are encompassed in moral injury, but developed as different themes by those living the reality. You will see many examples of this throughout Chapters 6 and 7.

From an academic standpoint, we see that betrayal is clearly part of moral injury, but the person experiencing it is reporting the betrayal as a separate experience. We are accepting this and focusing on our original intent, which is to honor what we are hearing from our colleagues. At the same time, we acknowledge that experts on these matters may see the themes we discuss organized differently. We acknowledge that we did not necessarily discover anything new; we just teased it apart and gave voice to those experiencing it.

Experts have long struggled with the understanding of where burnout ends and moral injury begins. Naturally, the individuals currently caught in the cross-fire and not spending their time in this academic space have an even more difficult time parsing it out. There appears to be strong overlap between burnout and moral injury. We do understand that burnout is fundamentally a demand-resource mismatch, while moral injury is a fundamental wound to one's core. We feel that drawing a line in the sand between them is unnecessary. They are both key to understanding what our colleagues revealed and, very often, are experienced in concert.

Our discussions with experts helped us recognize how to integrate the information from our participants within the current body of knowledge. We believe there is value in contributing this information for two reasons: (1) there is inherent value in hearing the stories directly from the individuals experiencing these phenomena and (2) it is of value to recognize that how the experts understand these phenomena is not the same as the way that the individual experiencing it will report what they are observing and feeling.

As we listened, five distinct themes emerged. Each theme has been given its own chapter. Our colleagues are feeling extreme pressure from every direction. As we reviewed the transcriptions and discussed the responses, we began to envision that each of these themes represents a vector of a containment unit that is continuously compressing the individual physician. Think Star Wars Episode IV and the scene in the trash compactor or perhaps a perpetually shrinking gelatinous cube. We call it "the squeeze."

CHAPTER 3

Loss
of Control

Loss of autonomy takes many forms. Most commonly, our interviewees reported the following: (1) loss of control over the *pace* at which they practice, (2) loss of control over *how* they practice, and (3) loss of control over *when* they practice.

Evidence of each of these phenomena were found in virtually every interview. How exactly they manifest depends on the demographic of the physician as an individual. For example, we might be talking to a middle-aged male cardiologist in a large academic institution, or a young mother who practices pediatrics in a rural setting for a large physician-owned group. The daily frustrations of these two people will be different. But the resulting emotional fallout is very similar.

In the following tables, we provide some of the quotes from our physician participants about how they have been stripped of autonomy in their practice and how this drives the pressures of "the squeeze."

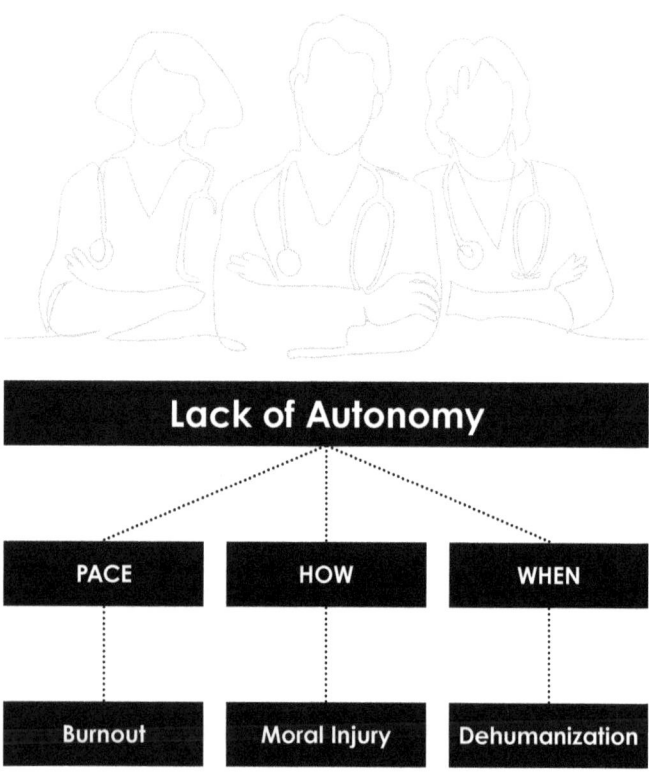

Loss of Autonomy Component	Physician Participant Quotes	Result
PACE	"…there was more pressure to see more patients, to go faster."	BURNOUT
	"I feel like I never really successfully launched my career, and I kept trying to be able to practice in a way that felt right to me, but I was really stifled and suffocated by the administration that I was working under, and I didn't have control over my schedule."	
	"Paperwork…the doubling of that paperwork… still squished into the same amount of time with the patient."	
	"… what I saw was… this top-down push. That we weren't doing enough. We needed to do better and… They just kept on… and then, if anybody left because they didn't like it, we were not replacing anybody. It was just like…more work for everybody who's left behind. But you still have to do it in a short amount of time. You still have to get it done without any errors."	

THE DOCTOR IS NO LONGER IN

Loss of Autonomy Component	Physician Participant Quotes	Result
HOW	"And it became very difficult despite all my best intentions to practice the way that I wanted to practice and be able to spend the time that I needed to with patients to give them good care and to have enough time in my life."	MORAL INJURY
	"I don't like to be told… how to be taking care of patients by some individual… in a three-piece suit and tie, sitting in some spacious office who never has set foot in the operating room. I don't need them to tell me how to how to manage my patients."	
	"But I think when I was being asked to do things that I felt put my patients in jeopardy or work against my own moral beliefs that I thought it may be time to walk away."	
	"Medicine is run by a lot of people who don't practice medicine. And as a result of that, we are unable to provide the kind of care we would provide because you know we all took the Hippocratic Oath. We all want to do no harm."	
	"And I saw that the… the standards also changed because they were getting paid… Without really seeing a lot of people, but it took away their autonomy. It took away their power. And the art of what they were doing, because now you had to… subscribe to hospital policy. You were an employee; you were not an independent practitioner."	

Loss of Autonomy Component	Physician Participant Quotes	Result
WHEN	"I think I recognized that I wasn't enjoying myself, that I just felt that I my life was not under my control and my time was not under my control."	DEHUMANIZATION
	"... I want to be a great mom and a great wife but how can I say no to my dying, cancer-stricken patients? And so... burnout is real. And part of it is self-inflicted, right? But it's there's no boundaries. We're not allowed to have boundaries. And if you do... when I try to have a boundary, they look at me like I'm doing something wrong... and then I become the problem doctor."	
	"I was trying to catch up on sleep. I was trying to catch up on billing, you know you're seeing you're overbooked and yet you know you're overbooked. And you know, I just dreaded that third week."	
	"My main priority was to preserve the quality of the visit with the patient and so everything else got pushed to my personal time right? So lunch and home is when I would do my notes and read the portal messages and follow up on results and respond to questions. And it got to a point where even the time with the patient was getting eroded."	

From these quotes, it is evident that these physicians were experiencing pressure in many ways. But there was one physician who felt *all* of them.

Her story is both striking and memorable, but also tragic in how unremarkable it sounds as we become inured to the way physicians are treated today. It is the story of a brilliant and incredibly caring critical care physician / trauma surgeon who specialized in ECMO. She had undergone years of extensive training and, until very recently, worked long hours at one of the largest and most prestigious hospitals in the country.

ECMO stands for "extra corporeal membrane oxygenation." ECMO is effectively a heart / lung bypass machine. It is a very tenuous and expensive treatment. The use of ECMO requires both complex clinical knowledge and considerable decision-making about which patients will benefit most from this precious and rare resource.

During the COVID pandemic, she was the one who had to make the difficult decision about who gets ECMO and a chance at life — and who does not. On the surface, this sounds like a terrible job, right?

But she told us that the clinical decision-making, the judgment about which patient was most likely to benefit, was actually the easy part. After all, that's the job. However, what was happening around her was *not* the job, and *is* ultimately what drove her away from medicine forever. She did this job around the clock for two years, on top of often being the ICU attending and operating, and everything else her job had always entailed. On several occasions, she was given "feedback" about certain decisions. These did not come from anyone who was willing to help do the job, but from people playing Monday morning quarterback. None of her partners stepped up to help. No adjustment of her other duties was offered by her leadership. Despite the additional hours and stress, no financial bonus was discussed. She did this for months while still doing her "day job." Everyone watched, and no one offered help. Nearly a year into this, she voiced her frustrations to her division chair about this intolerable situation. The response?

"Well ... why do you do this to yourself?"

Showing incredible strength, she continued this work until the pandemic was effectively over. Knowing that there was no one else willing to do the work, she stayed, showing her tremendous commitment to humanity and the oath that she took. Once the need had eased, she left medicine forever. Her personal qualities make her one of the most impressive physicians that we have ever encountered. Her skills are a gift to humanity, and they have been squandered.

The record of her exit may have you thinking that "COVID" was responsible. To this, we say emphatically that COVID did *not* do this to her. She was happy to do the work. If she had been thanked and supported, this could have been a defining career milestone in the other direction. She should have been exalted by a grateful community for her efforts. Had that occurred, she would almost certainly still be practicing. This would have been a memorable time during the early years of an illustrious career. Instead, she felt leaving medicine was the only option just six years after completing decades of training.

Had we supported this physician during the time of her Herculean efforts caring for patients with COVID, she probably would have continued to practice for another 30 to 40 years. She would have gained even greater skills. She would have shared those skills with upcoming physicians. She would have saved countless lives and trained others to save countless lives. We don't know that we can even quantify the loss of just this one physician. It is sobering to think that she is just 1 of about 70,000 physicians who have left (Vogel, 2023). This loss is staggering, for our profession, and for society at large.

We need to wrap our heads around this problem — and quickly. In the creation of this book, we have had the pleasure of getting to know Dr. Todd Otten. Dr. Otten is the author of *Ripple of Change*. In his book, Dr. Otten emphasizes that we all need to take responsibility for fixing our healthcare system (Otten & Judy, 2023). As things get worse, finger-pointing will become even more popular. But we must avoid this.

When we think about this wonderful ECMO specialist, it is easy to feel angry with her partners for not stepping up, and with her administration for not offering help, and so many more things. But her partners were also caught in this same system that takes and doesn't give back. Their lack of teamwork is evidence of a system with inadequate resources for physician support. Do we blame the administration for not providing enough money? Well … No. The hospital is running on a tight margin. They can't afford to give bonuses to every doctor who steps up. After all, she wasn't the only one working hard, right? And what about her division chair with the less-than-helpful comment: "Why do you do this to yourself?" While perhaps not his finest moment, we do not envy anyone who oversaw critical care teams during the pandemic. He was swamped with many other miserable and overworked physicians who were not getting what they needed, too. She was one of many. And it is doubtful that anyone was celebrating his efforts every day. So, who or what is to blame? How did we get here?

This story highlights multiple aspects of the phenomenon we are calling "the squeeze." In the U.S. right now, costs of our healthcare system are out of control. As discussed previously, many obstacles have been created to curb that cost. However, those obstacles have actually resulted in *increased* cost and decreased reimbursement. This has led to hospitals that are running on an ever-shrinking margin. In our fee-for-service system, a common method to keep revenue up is to increase "productivity" pressure on physicians. The executive leadership puts pressure on the clinical leadership, who then puts pressure on the physicians that provide direct care to patients. This has been worsening over time, but COVID amplified this until we got to the point where physicians are at their breaking point. In the following chapters, we will share how this pressure has manifested among our participants, and how each of these themes contributes to the "squeeze."

"It was a gradual decline, but it was getting to the point where it started to impact my physical health, where I was like, I can't... I can't sleep, I can't eat anymore. My romantic relationship is being very hurt by this. I feel miserable at work and miserable at home. I just feel miserable all the time. I'm working really hard. And you know, I'm taking medication. I'm doing therapy. Nothing is working. I think it was just that moment where I was like I am not functioning, and this has been a very slow decline but has lasted a really long time and ... I don't want to live like this anymore ... And there are things that are more important to me than my job, and that includes my physical health, my mental health, my friendships, my partnership. And. I can't do this... like this anymore."

This quote from one of our participants demonstrates how our fellow physicians are experiencing the squeeze on an interpersonal level (meaning, how the external world is impacting them). Doctors are human. Over time, those external forces become internalized. How are

THE DOCTOR IS NO LONGER **IN**

these individuals experiencing the effects of these external pressures on an intrapersonal level?

CHAPTER 4

Burnout

Nearly every one of our interviewees reported experiencing burnout. Many of them described themselves as "burnt to a crisp," meaning unable to come back from this burnout. Burnout can be a transient experience. People can step away or change the conditions of the workplace and experience alleviation of the symptoms. However, if it goes on and on, people can be burnt to a crisp and simply cannot endure any more of the experience. That was definitely something that we heard many times (and both have experienced ourselves).

We asked each interviewee *how* they experienced burnout. We got different answers. Some experience burnout most in the psychological realm, with emotional exhaustion and the inability to get out of bed. We heard the word "dread" over and over. Other people experienced it more somatically, with physical exhaustion, sluggishness, tension headaches, and pain. Finally, some experienced it as behavioral issues in themselves. They found themselves to be irritable and thinking "this is not who I am." They reported feeling angry at patients when that would never have been the case previously. They felt like they were losing who they were at the core. We also had one interviewee who simply said,

> *"I don't see the difference between burnout and depression. For me, the experiences are exactly the same."*

This quote will likely resonate with some physician readers. It also brings up some of the issues with the term. Most of us who experience burnout are not spending significant amounts of time in the academic space around burnout. The descriptions of the experience and the literature around the issue don't always completely match. Despite this imperfect overlapping, burnout is a common term and quickly orients individuals to what we are discussing. For this reason, it will continue to be used and, given the current trajectory, will be used often. However, we need to remain cognizant that how one person is using that word may or may not directly correlate with the textbook definition (Maslach & Leiter, 2016; Shanafelt, 2018).

WHAT IS THE DEFINITION OF BURNOUT?

According to the World Health Organization (WHO), burnout is a syndrome that is conceptualized from chronic workplace stress that has not been successfully managed. It is characterized by 3 dimensions (World Health Organization: WHO, 2019):

1. Feelings of energy depletion or exhaustion
2. Increased mental distance from one's job or feelings of negativism or cynicism related to one's job
3. Reduced professional efficacy

Burnout refers specifically to phenomena in the occupational context and should not be applied to describe experiences in other areas of life.

We frequently hear about the role of resilience in combating burnout. Physician wellness committees across the county, albeit well-intentioned, may be making the blade of resentment sharper by putting the onus of "wellness" on the individual. Yoga, meditation, mindfulness — these are valuable and helpful practices. But the likelihood is that the people who made it through the rigors of medical school and residency are already relatively resilient human beings. To suggest that an individual simply lean into that even more when its wellspring is depleted is, well, insulting. Especially when the problem is not necessarily within the clinician; it is our large broken healthcare system. Resilience often comes from identifying things you can change, but when the things that need to be changed are outside of your control, the feeling of helplessness creeps in. When describing the experience of burnout, one of our participants stated,

> ***"I'm being held accountable for systems I don't own or control..."***

In the previous chapter about the lack of autonomy in clinical practice, we proposed that the lack of control regarding timing and pace of seeing patients, performing procedures, and other ways of delivering direct care, is central to the development of burnout. Time is this vastly and rapidly dwindling resource available to the physician in clinical care today. In the time that a physician has allocated to patient care, they are also expected to clear their inbox, accomplish administrative tasks, complete all necessary documentation, engage in 20 to 40 patient encounters like it's the first and only one of the day, precisely, safely and efficiently perform the maximum number of surgical cases that can be squeezed in during an OR day, perform thoughtful and meaningful leadership duties, and throughout it all, be pleasant to work with.

The problem is there just isn't enough time to accomplish all these tasks within a humanly possible time frame, so more gets squeezed into what time does exist and the rest spills over into time that wasn't initially meant for clinical work (dinner, bedtime with the kids, date night with a significant other, etc.). Physicians often refer to this as "pajama time."

> ***"Pajama time was just getting longer and longer, until all I did was work."***

Some even feel the strain of time to do basic human things.

> ***"I mean, I do take bathroom breaks, but you know, feeling bad about it because I have, you know, double-booked patients back-to-back."***

This grinding pace becomes more difficult when the goals for working like this become questionable. One participant said:

> *"...it's another thing if I'm following bureaucratic rules that aren't well thought out to maximize profit for a health care company that is trying to move as many patients through the door, as opposed to making sure that their outcomes are right. And so, to me, the general thing I would say is just lack of agency over my own time from a work-life balance perspective. But more importantly over my time even during the day, right? Like my schedule is not 16 to 20 patients that necessarily need to be seen, and [I] have a certain amount of time based on what they need. It's based on the system's needs, and how many new patients they've decided to contract with and what that means from a bonus perspective for CEOs and what have you."*

The grinding pace also leads to burnout in other ways, notably creating a barrier to human connection among staff, as well as with patients. Our participants put it best:

> *"And that connection that we might have to our residents, or our MAs or nurses, nursing staff ... is gone because*

there's no time to be human, you know, during that kind of thing. So burnout for me is sort of ... the lack of interaction and the lack of time, for the other stuff of healing that needs to happen, like communication, like touch, like time."

"You are so driven by the system to see as many patients, treat as many patients as humanly possible in a day that interacting with patients almost becomes an inconvenience because it slows you down. And it means you're not doing right by the patient by doing so. But there's just so much expected of you that you can't stop for a second."

"Burnout for me is, there's all these things I want to do that I can't do, but I have to do all these repetitive tasks... that aren't necessarily improving care, aren't efficient, and don't help me take care of all the other things I need to take care of."

Staffing continues to be an issue, so more tasks that weren't initially meant for physicians become our responsibility. Everyone we interviewed talked about this incessant and overwhelming pressure to do more. But not just "do more." Do more with less time, less staff, less financial resources, and less support. The message is: do more with less. Our physicians talked about getting squeezed until, ***"I'm like a tattered rag that simply has nothing left to give."***

Arm-in-arm with the message to "do more with less" is the message that whatever you're doing, however hard you are working, it is not enough. It feels it will never be enough and more will continuously be required. Many of our participants conveyed this grinding feeling of never being able to meet expectations, not because they were incapable or inadequate, but because the expectations were impossible. When you're staring down a barrel with no end, when there is no light at the end of an infinite tunnel, that's when despair takes root. Our participants described it in these ways:

> ***"I have given everything,
> and there is nothing left,
> and instead of saying thank you,
> we appreciate you, they're just asking,
> how can you give more? How can you
> give more, and how can you give more…"***

"There are some individuals who ... they've just gotten tired of showing up to the same ... You know it's the same treadmill every day and ...they're gradually increasing the slope of the treadmill, and you have to walk up the whole time and ... Administrators are just not... They're just not willing to listen. They're like, well, you, you just need to be more productive. You need to see more patients during your clinic."

This simply is not sustainable. Many of the physicians we interviewed were acutely aware of this. Some were able to see the imminent end of their own human capabilities:

"I'll be in practice for 15 years, and I know with 100% certainty that I do not have until age 65 to do what I'm currently doing."

THE DOCTOR IS NO LONGER IN

> *"It's not sustainable physically, because you know, medical records being electronic and patients having access and however many patients they put on during the day, that's only the tip of the iceberg in terms of the things you need to get done each day before, you know, you can go home. And that means an hour or two before work and an hour or two after, where you're answering emails..."*

Many of our colleagues reported that they had tried multiple times to talk to their leadership and tried to make their clinical environment safer and healthier for both patients and team members.

> *"But the bottom line always won. I couldn't get our leadership to see the mutual benefits. What's worse is that I always walked out of those meetings feeling guilty and inadequate."*

> *"All of these administrators know nothing about health care or read about it in a textbook. They don't know what goes on in patients' rooms. But, when we try to tell them, it falls on deaf ears."*

Many interviewees felt like they were emotionally manipulated to give more than they could comfortably give:

> *"My main priority was to preserve the quality of the visit with the patient and so everything else got pushed to my personal time, right? So, lunch and home is when I would do my notes and read the portal messages and follow up on results and respond to questions. And it got to a point where even the time with the patient was getting eroded."*

> *"I felt like I was being charged a 'passion tax.' My partners who cared less just didn't do it, but I couldn't leave it that way. So, you know ... I pick up the pieces, or pay the price or whatever."*

"... as if my passion for patient care was used against me until I had nothing left to give, and then I was discarded."

And so we end up with:

"I realized that I wanted to do something in healthcare to help people and that in order to do that in a sustainable way, I had to find another way besides bedside clinical medicine."

"We can only endure so much."

CHAPTER 5

Dehumanization: Cogs Don't Have Needs

" 'I called my department chief, and I said, 'I'm really struggling. I need to go see somebody.' And she said, 'I'm sorry. There's nobody here to take over for you.' So I was like, 'but I'm really struggling.' ... I'm crying on rounds, and I went to pronounce somebody dead on the roof, and I was crying ... I need help. But I just kept working. Later, they gave me an hour off to call EAP and I called. EAP, the number they gave me, he gave me three psychiatrists. And of the three, two were dead. So I mean, I'm trying to get help for myself. I'm trying so hard, incredibly hard."

THE DOCTOR IS NO LONGER IN

Human cultures churn around concepts of health and illness. The way in which human groups understand what it means to be "healthy" and "sick" are central to the fabric of what it means to be human. These definitions and understandings of health and illness vary throughout time and space, and this, in turn, drives how we respond to illness, how we treat illness, and how we know when we are healthy. This central and dynamic role of health and illness also shapes how we interact with those who facilitate our health and battle illness on our behalf.

One of the physicians we interviewed noted that being a physician was the most noble profession they could think of, second only to a priest. Without taking on delusions of grandeur, one could argue there may be some similarity. Priests are often seen as the gateways to "God," and the gatekeepers to salvation. Likewise, physicians and healers are often seen as gateways to health, and gatekeepers to cures and remedies for whatever it is that ails you. Both professions represent a body of knowledge that is historically inaccessible to the common person. Sometimes this is so much so that priests and healers occupy one and the same body, as treatments are both medicinal and spiritual.

Dehumanization: Cogs Don't Have Needs

One of us (Dr. Rieth) was fortunate to spend some time in a Tibetan prefecture in southwest China many years ago. She worked with Tibetan monks and doctors to understand how the two spheres of existence, the physical and the spiritual, intertwine in the way they practice medicine. The lesson learned was that the division between the physical and spiritual is not universal and perhaps not entirely true. One could easily witness the fluidity between medicinal remedies and spiritual practice for addressing the same ailment. The practitioners, both monk and doctor, partake in this practice as members of their communities, as active cultural participants. In doing so, they bring a humanity to the interaction with their patients that is met with relief, comfort, and understanding. This context conveys the sentiment from a patient's perspective that "you are a person, I am a person, we both believe that you are trying to help me in ways that we both understand."

Zoom out and over to the United States. Our practice of medicine — how we understand health and illness, what causes illness, how we treat illness — is arguably quite different from that spot on the Tibetan steppe. However, the same basic tenets exist.

Part of the "nobility" of our careers is derived from that human connection that opens the gateway to remedy, to overcoming disease, and to the better health that is so central to our identity. (Interestingly, the American health mindset is very illness-centric, and "health" is often defined as the "absence of illness.") So many of the physicians we spoke with mentioned how, in the beginning, they felt medicine was a great calling and it dovetailed beautifully with their love of taking care of patients. ***"I got into medicine because I wanted to feel like I was making the world a better place and helping people."*** Then, they start practicing in the real world of the American healthcare system.

Cog ['kag] (*noun*): 1. A tooth on the rim of a wheel or gear. 2. A subordinate but integral person or part.

For many physicians we talked with, this humanity and human connection coupled with the desire and expectation that they would be "doing good" in their careers sets the bar quite high. Some argue that this deep-seated altruism leads to unrealistic expectations and a sense of guilt for not doing enough. Physicians tend to be extremely driven and self-motivated. We take the job seriously, and we end up having to sacrifice other things in our lives to be able to feel like we are accomplishing these goals of "doing good" in providing medical and surgical care. The physicians we interviewed universally spoke about giving and sacrificing to the point that it hurt. It hurt mentally. It hurt physically. It hurt socially. It hurt family relationships and parenting relationships. It hurt spousal relationships.

>*"Giving 1,000% all the time became exhausting."*

>*"You are pronouncing people dead when you haven't slept for three days. You're trying to be empathetic when you can't keep your eyes open, you have five patients who are dying. Somebody shot themselves in the face. You're running down to the OR to help the anesthesiologist, because they need help while someone is dying on the floor, like there was not enough of me to go around."*

And for some, it hurt physically.

"...to the point where I would be at the pool, and I couldn't even relax because I'm looking to see if someone has drowned. I'm at a baseball field and I'm looking for the AED, and I'm running a code in my head of how I'm going to resuscitate a kid ... I started feeling my heart racing in my ear, and I started feeling nauseated, and I thought maybe I drank too much coffee that day and then I didn't feel well all day, and I was just, like, always about to cry, I was always on the verge of tears."

And when it comes to the point of needing help, of needing to be treated like a human being in the same way we treat others, therein lies the betrayal by our institutions. Our clinical productivity (and hence our apparent value to our employer) takes a hit when we need to take bereavement time. Because no one can plan these kinds of things, they are last-minute requests that evoke a punitive response. When a physician needs to take maternity leave, the first thoughts from colleagues and leadership are about who will cover that individual's time on the work schedule, or how that time will be repaid.

Dehumanization: Cogs Don't Have Needs

When tragedies among our own occur, the first questions are about who will cover that person's patients? That *person*. Yes, they are / were a person, who gave 1,000% until it hurt, and for some reason, this person is deprived of the human qualities and dignity that we otherwise willingly provide to everyone else. This is part of the dehumanizing process.

We want to make a distinction here between dehumanization and depersonalization. Depersonalization is often identified as a component of burnout and refers to the experience of becoming more negative, cynical, and impersonal in one's interactions with other people, including patients. This has more to do with what physicians experience internally in the process of becoming and being burned out. In contrast, dehumanization is the process of depriving a person of human qualities, personality, or dignity. This is something that is *done to* physicians in the current practice context. This is what physicians experience when they realize that their human qualities are not the interest of their employers and institutions. Rather, it is the ability to keep working, to grind on, to produce more units that can be valued with a dollar amount, and to persevere in the role of cog on this wheel of "health care."

For those keeping the books, this is a convenient way of viewing the physician workforce, because cogs don't have personal needs.

Some of the doctors who shared their stories talked about feeling like their humanness created burdens for everyone else. As mentioned earlier, for some, this occurred with life events, such as death in the family or maternity, or with the sudden loss of a co-worker. But they also talked about being made to feel completely replaceable, and this is a process that occurred more on a daily basis. A slow and steady sanding away of human qualities until you wake up one day, and you're just a smooth little cog nicely grinding away in a machine whose goal it is, ultimately, to be profitable. When you no longer are seen for your individual, unique and valuable attributes, you become replaceable by another physician conformed into a cog that will fit just as well into the space you thought you occupied in a special way.

> ***"I feel like I've started out more as an individual, and I'm now a commodity, that, you know, this doctor equals that much productivity."***

"I think we're coming to a crossroads between commoditization of people as resources, and the joy of medicine for individual providers…"

"It's just become so much of a business model that it all doesn't feel personal anymore."

"… you realize all the sacrifices that you made. It doesn't matter, because in the end you're just replaceable, you know? I always thought like, oh, I'm being so heroic and sacrificing this and that and for what? You go, you leave, and the next doctor comes in … everyone's replaceable. That compassion for doctors or treating us like human beings is not there. We're just work horses. A number. And that's hard to conceptually wrap your head around."

We mentioned Dr. Carrie Cunningham earlier in this book. She was the president of the Association of Academic Surgery (AAS) the same year that our research was being performed.

THE DOCTOR IS NO LONGER IN

In her outgoing presidential address, she courageously shared her personal story of mental health issues and the story of how she lost her close friend and colleague, Dr. Christina Barkley, to suicide (Academic Surgical Congress & Cunningham, 2023). You can view this presidential address on various websites, including YouTube. If you do, you may notice in one of her slides a photo of a coffee mug. She had it made after it all went down.

The mug's script:
I ♥ sharp edges

She goes on to explain that our system is systematically sanding down the rough edges of its human resources. The system tries to sand down our rough edges, so that we will fit the mold and make better cogs. Part of this molding process can be seen in the wording used to refer to physicians, a term that historically held respect. The term "physicians" is now interchangeable with "providers," grouping us in with other types of healthcare professionals so that we are all now treated like cogs. But it's important to remember that the sharp edges are what makes us unique. They should not be sanded down.

Part of an individual's uniqueness may come from their role as a parent. Let's look at the experiences of active parent physicians through one of our participants, a busy surgeon. She shared her own story, and it started with a tale about her senior male partner at the hospital. She started, ***"You know how old men like to tell stories? But, not new stories. They like to tell the same stories over and over..."***

At the institution where she had previously worked, there was a senior white male surgeon, and he had three stories he liked to tell. One of them, that was heard numerous times, was about a time years ago when his in-laws became very ill in Florida, and his wife had to leave town for a few months, leaving him essentially a single father with four children. The most striking part about this story was that he remembered this time *fondly*.

He described how he cut his clinic time back, to put the kids on the bus in the morning. He changed his OR schedule to ensure that he could attend their various school functions. He changed how his nurses functioned, to allow them to assist patients with advanced needs. He went on and on. The most remarkable thing about this story is how much autonomy he had during that time, which could have otherwise been incredibly difficult. So much so, that he always ended the story by saying, "I'm so glad that happened, because I got to have that precious time with my kids that I wouldn't have had otherwise."

Forty years later, our young, female physician in the same department abruptly became a single parent. The result was very different — she no longer practices clinical medicine. She attempted to shift clinic hours, but that was not an option. She tried to establish block time, but that was unavailable. She suggested seeing fewer patients in the office and instead doubling up her time on the call schedule, allowing a structured schedule for childcare planning. But that was denied. There is simply no (longer a) way to be a single parent in that same position today.

That is how different things have become. The same options that had allowed him to be a single parent, and even enjoy that time, are no longer available in the current climate. We used to value physicians enough that we would say, "Yes, Dr. Sapien, of course we will work with you. You are of tremendous value to this team and this institution." Now, the response is, "I'm sorry, Dr. Cog, but that simply won't do."

Dehumanization: Cogs Don't Have Needs

When you compare the two experiences, yes, there is frustration and questions about the role of gender. Yet there is no villain. The system has simply changed. What the system can now tolerate in terms of physician-needs is down to zero. The system, as it is currently designed, relies on doctors with the following criteria:

- No needs
- No lived experiences
- No varying schedules
- No bad days
- No errors
- No emotions

These criteria are simply not sustainable for human physicians. Instead, we now have more physicians leaving, more physicians dying by suicide, more physicians with addiction, more physicians getting divorced, etc. More and more ruined lives, across all demographics. But, as is so often the case, some demographics suffer more than others.

If all the physicians in the U.S. were leaving direct patient care at the same rate, we would expect the demographic ratios of the physicians leaving to match the demographic ratios of the physicians staying.

It is probably not a surprise to anyone that this is not the case. In our participant group, the physicians with whom we spoke were 2:1 female and many were people of color, immigrants, and / or with other variations of lived experience, including a history of childhood poverty, disability, etc. It seems that those who don't "fit the mold" are more likely to leave. In fact, the available information from the AMA, National Institute of Health (NIH), and American Association of Medical Colleges (AAMC) indicates that underrepresented minority physicians face distinct challenges, such as discrimination, lack of professional support, and systemic barriers in their career trajectories, all of which lead to higher rates of burnout, career dissatisfaction, and ultimately attrition (Adebayo et al., 2021).

The issues highlighted above affect all physicians. As mentioned previously, there were twice as many females compared to males in our sample for this project. This reflects what is happening broadly in this country. Data from the AMA and other organizations show female physicians have higher rates of burnout compared to their male counterparts and are more likely to report job dissatisfaction and consider leaving medicine due to burnout. Female physicians are also more likely than male physicians to report work-life balance as a significant issue, contributing to their decisions to leave clinical practice. Female physicians are more likely to take on a larger share of household and childcare responsibilities, which impacts their career choices, such as leaving clinical practice (Paturel, 2022; Frank et al., 2019; Ligibel et al., 2023). This issue is the subject of numerous books and journal articles already, but we bring it up here to acknowledge the impact it has for our participants. Some reported specific incidents, such as:

> *"…after a patient coded in the operating room, my residents were like 'why was nobody listening to you when you were telling them what to do?' Recognizing that they just weren't listening to me because in large part, I was a woman, and they didn't respect me the same way that they would have just immediately respected one of my male colleagues."*

Many of our female participants mentioned the role of gender in broader terms regarding their frustration with clinical practice:

"My marriage was on the rocks ... I was never home. I was always stressed. I had, like, an incredible work burden ... you know, I think there was an expectation that I was supposed to be the mother and the doctor, you know, bring money in and do the childcare and be a household manager."

"At this point, it doesn't even feel like I'm going to have my own children and my own husband at my deathbed, because I just feel like they don't know me. When I walk down the stairs in the morning my kids say, 'bye, mom.' That's the first reaction. It's not 'good morning.' It's not 'hello.' They know. I've come down in my scrubs, and it's time for mom to leave, and mom won't be back until after dinner and may or may not participate in bedtime."

Dehumanization: Cogs Don't Have Needs

"...my female residents feel like they have to work twice as hard to do the same thing. Because every time they do something, six people ask them to justify why they've made that decision, or why they've made that request and in hearing that from them I realized that that is happening to me all the time."

"I was working under a very senior surgeon who was male, and I'm a younger female, and I don't think he meant to do it on purpose, but I think he really wanted me to be the damsel in distress because then he could come in and be the white knight."

"But I think there's so much damage done, especially to women in our training, because we're just constantly given the message that we're not good enough and that you have to do better and that nothing short of perfection is acceptable."

Are we surprised by any of these quotes? We shouldn't be.

Our society doesn't value people equally, despite our national ethos of equality for all. This is also true for physicians. We don't value all physicians equally. As the squeeze gets tighter, some physicians feel it more than others. Who feels the squeeze more? Perhaps not surprisingly:

- Women
- People of color
- Immigrants
- People who represent the LGBTQ+ community
- Anyone with any kind of disability
- Anyone who has to check "other" when describing themselves

There are limitless variations of lived experience and not all have been listed here. Simply put, it is important to recognize that any variation of lived experience away from the "default" seems to be a risk factor for leaving. Not only is this unfortunate, but there is also a much bigger problem that may not be immediately obvious.

We already have well-founded data to show that the physician workforce should match the population being served as much as possible, because that improves patient outcomes (Adebayo et al., 2021; Silver et al., 2019). If we took a community and lined up all the people / would-be patients and put a mirror in front of them, their doctors should "look" like them. This is the goal, because it optimizes patient outcomes. Therefore, if we lose diversity in the physician workforce, we can expect worse outcomes for patients. This is in addition to the worse outcomes of not having enough doctors or having doctors who are stressed out and don't have the resources they need. Simply put, not all physicians are regarded with the same respect, and this has major implications for who gets what they need to do the job well.

As we began to recognize these phenomena, we tried to talk to key stakeholders at higher levels within large hospital systems. There was a pretty significant blind spot to these problems, which is very familiar in systems where those in power don't, or won't, recognize what is occurring and will even diminish or negate the experience.

We feel that physicians who are currently on the front lines of patient care will likely resonate with the content of this book. After some promotional interviews for the book were broadcast, we heard many affirmative responses and statements from doctors like, "Yes, that! That is exactly what's happening. Thank you so much for giving voice to my experience." Conversely, physicians at higher levels (executive and administrative leadership positions) often argued about whether this is truly occurring — whether physicians are unhappy and leaving. We were accused of being dramatic, hyperbolic, and even disingenuous. Perhaps, this is a confirmation of what is occurring. Like most broken systems, the people who are being affected are very clear on what is occurring, while those in positions of power cannot see the problem, or feel unable to change it and turn a blind eye.

CHAPTER 6

Moral Injury

"I had been slowly burning out for several years. My distress significantly worsened as pushback became more common and encumbered quality patient care."

One of our participants, a Gyn Oncologist, described how she met a new patient with stage 3 ovarian cancer and scheduled an open abdominal surgery followed by chemotherapy, consistent with the standard of care. This time, it wasn't the insurance company that gave her pushback; it was the hospital. They wanted her to use the robot, which would take less time and allow the hospital to charge more. She wasn't comfortable documenting that she had resected all bulk disease (which is the standard of care) with the robot, because she felt it did not provide the adequate tactile feedback necessary for accomplishing that goal.

She went on to tell us how it felt as though her options were to either (1) use the robot and lie or (2) perform the planned open surgery and deal with the lack of support for the patient's "prolonged" stay after the surgery (several days instead of just an overnight). Not only was this surgeon's plan making less revenue, it was also costing the hospital more. But she felt that, until she had solid data stating otherwise, she was not going to risk her patient's overall survival for short-term outcomes.

The insurance companies and the hospital did not seem interested in our participant's goals. The "feedback" sessions became more frequent. When she didn't fall in line, the resources to safely perform her planned surgeries were less available. Several complications occurred, and they had the ammunition they needed to put her on the defensive. From there, it got very uncomfortable. She felt she was walking on eggshells while trying to carry her patients, and ultimately, she didn't feel safe anymore.

Her son's health issues and struggles at home provided an opportunity to walk away in a socially acceptable manner. It was months before she could begin to recognize what had happened. A friend sent her an article on moral injury. She immediately felt validated and the healing began (Dean et al., 2020).

What is moral injury? Sometimes, people think that it is just physicians being whiny. But a physician with moral injury is *not* a doctor with "hurt feelings." A physician with moral injury is a person who feels morally compromised, so much so that they can't participate in the injustice anymore. In her book, *If I Betray These Words*, Dr. Wendy Dean teaches us that moral injury is defined as "perpetrating, failure to prevent, bearing witness to, or learning about acts that transgress deeply held moral beliefs and expectations" (Dean, et al, 2020; Dean & Talbot, 2023). It is a thoughtfully written book, with full stories from or about physicians.

In this book, Dr. Dean dedicates a chapter to the story of a physician named Hannah. The chapter ends by saying, "Everywhere Hannah has worked for the past decade has forsaken patients in the name of profit and betrayed physicians trying to practice according to their training … They are all using the same shareholder primacy playbook from business school and getting the same tragic results. As a result of this misplaced focus, medicine is rapidly losing clinicians like Hannah and her partners, who refuse to practice first for profits and then for patients."

The physicians that we interviewed used some of the following words to describe their experiences with moral injury:

"I was not able to provide the quality of care that my patients deserve."

"They deserve better, but I wasn't able to make the system work for them."

"It feels terrible to be forced to provide substandard care. I couldn't do it anymore."

"I couldn't be put in situations where I was forced to provide care for my patients that I wouldn't want for my own loved ones."

"I remember a time when I was able to provide patient care with all my heart and both of my hands. Then, it was with one hand tied behind my back. Then, with two hands tied behind my back. Now, it's with both hands tied behind my back and in the dark. I can't do it anymore."

Moral injury also seemed to be very closely related to a dysphoria between the anticipated joy of helping people versus the reality of patient care:

"I got into this to help people, but that's not what I found."

"This isn't why I went into medicine."

"That's not how I imagined it would be. I thought you'd have some real conversations about risks, benefits of surgeries and get to know your patients a little bit and sort of treat the whole patient, whole human instead of just the disease process."

THE DOCTOR IS NO LONGER IN

"When I chose to become a doctor, I thought that caring for my fellow man was second only to priesthood. Now, it just feels ... greedy ... or soiled somehow."

We spoke with a cardiologist who has been practicing for 20 years. He remembers a time when his schedule was filled with patients who truly required his care. When he identified a patient in need of an echocardiogram (an ultrasound of the heart), he was able to get the study performed on the same day. Now, many of the patients that need him have the "wrong" insurance. There are no slots in his schedule for "those patients." Instead, his day is filled with the worried well who have insurance that pays for extra visits. And the patients that truly need him? He must use his time after work at night and on weekends to track them down by phone and see how they are doing. And a same day echocardiogram? No longer an option. He has brought up all these concerns with his administration countless times. But there is always a financial reason why this can't be improved. And what do you think happened when a patient of his suffered a heart attack at home? Let's just say that our poor friend, Dr. X, was given some "feedback" about trying to care for patients over the phone.

We saw this phenomenon across all specialties. Everyone we spoke with had stories to tell. They knew what their patients needed, but "the system" was preventing them from establishing that treatment plan. A central part of this problem is trying to deliver care through insurance companies. For many physicians, arguing with insurance companies to justify why they want to do something for a patient is maddening. We often must complete forms called "prior authorization." Other times, we must participate in conversations called a "peer-to-peer." This is usually a phone call with another physician who works for the insurance company. This physician is rarely from your specialty and simply is not aware of the details of the standards in that field. You are then required to explain to a colleague the data and educate them. It can be long and exhausting, and it is always inconvenient. Sometimes, it takes many rounds of this just to get one procedure approved, even for medically straightforward procedures. It is staggering at times the additional time, effort, and frustration required to try and get a patient the care you feel is medically necessary and appropriate. And this process is often still unsuccessful.

In one case, an interviewee was arguing with an insurance company that his patient needed a cardiac ablation for a very standard medical condition in which cardiac ablation is an accepted standard treatment. The first hurdle with the patient's insurance company was an online form. There was then a long email exchange. It took a while, but he finally realized that he was arguing *with a robot*. That's right. The insurance company has employed AI technology to come between you and your physician. This is the level of insanity at which we now find ourselves. This instance adds insult to moral injury by not even allowing the physician to discuss this case with a human fellow physician.

Our stories were all collected anonymously. However, there is a story that has already been told publicly, well over a decade ago, that could have easily been one of our interviewees. This story sounds very much like every interview we conducted. Because this story is already public, we can share it with you. It is quite representative of what we heard (version taken from Makary, 2018).

> Dr. Guy Clifton was one of the busiest neurosurgeons at a leading Houston hospital. He was a distinguished chairman

and a powerful figure there. He would frequently call upon his hospital's administrators to address the safety concerns of his staff. For example, as the practice of hand-washing gained attention in health care, he noticed that there were not enough sinks for his staff to wash their hands in the ICU. He had blueprints drawn to put in more sinks, but repeatedly his ideas were not funded by his administration. He also pushed to digitize X-rays, arguing that digital access would decrease the number of X-rays that would need to be repeated, but this request was also denied.

There was one issue that Dr. Clifton was most passionate about fixing: the high postsurgical complication rate he observed in the ICU. He noticed high ICU nurse turnover, which correlated with the high complication rate. The safety culture was poor, and the structure of the nursing coverage was a growing safety hazard and part of patients having longer ICU stays. Dr. Clifton devised a plan to restructure the ICU, but this was, again, denied. Frustrated with the resistance to his ideas based on his experience and feedback from colleagues on the front lines of care, he resigned. He realized that hospitals get more money for each complication, X-ray, and extra patient day in the ICU. One well-known national study that was, ironically, released around the time of his departure estimated that a hospital gets paid $10,000 extra per surgical complication (Dimick et al., 2006). He then understood that the hospital's rationale of not having a "business case" for these changes did not align with his own values.

At the time, there wasn't a term for what Dr. Clifton experienced. Today, we call this moral injury, and it is one the main reasons that we are losing physicians in droves.

Many of our interviewees talked about wanting to continue to use their skills for patient benefit, that they were not giving up on their patients despite needing to leave direct patient care. In Dr. Clifton's case, he decided to take the message to a broader audience and worked on Capitol Hill, dedicating his life to reforming health care in a nonpartisan way. The message was simple: financially rewarding bad medicine is endemic in American health care. He wrote a book titled

Flatlined: Resuscitating American Medicine, which outlined the perverse incentives of our health care system. As a testament to what one doctor can do when he is willing to take a bold step, Dr. Clifton is having an impact on the national conversation on health care (Clifton, 2008).

His principled departure from that hospital in Houston had a big impact there. The hospital lost millions of dollars in revenue from his absence. His cause there was taken up by his colleague, neurosurgeon Dong Kim, who refused to serve as chief unless the administration delivered on Dr. Clifton's requests to fix the hospital's problems. The hospital's administration, in desperate need of a new leader to rescue the department, finally granted Dr. Kim his request. In a radical turnaround, the administrators listened to each safety concern and asked how they could fix it. A new ICU was built (with plenty of sinks for employees to wash their hands). The nursing care was reorganized, and new nurses were hired for the unit. The teamwork culture improved. Nurses wanted to work there again, and there was less turnover. Morale was markedly better, and postsurgical complications decreased. The average patient stay in the ICU was reduced safely. Patients' medical bills reflected the lower cost of safer care. This hospital is now considered by many in the field to be one of the top five neurosurgery centers in the United States.

Dr. Clifton's story took place nearly 20 years ago and shows us how one physician tried to curb costs while improving patient outcomes. In some institutional attempts to curb costs, we have placed emphasis on some short-term outcomes in lieu of the "big picture."

We are now seeing a new, related problem arguably rooted in a deeper distrust of the healthcare system at large: the erosion of patients' trust in their doctors. Patients now have unhindered access to variable quality information, misinformation, and disinformation on the internet and social media. As a result, many physicians find themselves in difficult situations where patients' perceptions may impede their ability to provide good care. For example, we now have online reviews reporting whether or not Dr. X is a "5-star" physician. We understand that the idea is to see what kind of bedside manner other patients experienced. What we can't tell from this review, however, is whether the person who gave 0 stars received quality care. It is entirely possible they received very good medical care, but it did not necessarily make them happy. Does the 5-star review give us truly helpful feedback? Does that 0-star review make Dr. X a bad doctor?

All these things that we are measuring, are they really measuring good or bad medicine? They are not. They are a slippery slope for creating perverse incentives to do things that are antithetical to good medicine, and we find ourselves in these situations all the time. We talked to frustrated physicians who said:

> ***"I'm not a drug dealer."***

> ***"Dude, I'm not a Starbucks."***

> ***"This isn't a Burger King. You can't always have it your way."***

THE DOCTOR IS NO LONGER IN

"You know, medicine is turning into this consumer service, right? It's a service industry at this point. And so we have a bunch of ... not milestones, but, like, ways of being evaluated outside of our medical and technical expertise that affect our reimbursement, that then affect the kind of patients that we end up seeing ... which then has downstream consequences."

Many of them recounted stories where they were admonished by the hospital administration for less than 5-star reviews in settings where they had clearly delivered good medicine.

One such doctor was running an Urgent Care in a community where the opioid crisis is particularly bad. Many people presented seeking prescriptions that were simply inappropriate. She had a "less than 5-star" review, again. She was called into the administrator's office for discussion and possible remediation. ***"He was drug seeking,"*** was her defense. The administrator's reply: ***"Then just give him the drugs."***

She quit that day. She is never returning to medicine. Last we heard, she was on a yoga retreat and has changed her lifestyle significantly to both maintain her sanity and her decreased household income. She is much healthier and happier. She told us that the "golden handcuffs" were getting uncomfortably tight, and it just wasn't worth it anymore. The theme of fear of lost wages also came up in nearly every interview and the term "golden handcuffs" emerged several times. There are many physicians who feel trapped in the system, but can't imagine leaving direct patient care and risking the loss of income. This fear for their personal finances often worsens the moral injury.

> ***"It used to mean that 'selling out' was leaving medicine and doing something else. Today, I feel like I am 'selling out' by staying in this system and remaining complicit in the injustice."***

CHAPTER 7

Trust and Betrayal

While drinking coffee and checking LinkedIn messages, up pops a post from Dr. Bryce Bowers. Dr. Bowers is the founder of Badge of Burnout. He is wearing antlers and buffalo plaid. The post says, "#1 reason I left medicine: lack of honesty" (Bowers, 2023).

He is not alone in this sentiment. This came up so consistently that we have dedicated an entire chapter to this problem.

If you see a physician resign with little or no notice and / or no future plan, we almost guarantee that a breach of trust is an important part of that story. This is also true if you see a group of doctors leave simultaneously. What we found is that the constant crank of working when you are told, seeing more patients, and being told how to care for them, are the slow burn of the burnout. But the final straw is often a major breach of trust.

We heard terrible stories of scapegoating and sham remediations; both a means for the hospital system to distance themselves from ownership of issues and offer the physician up as a scapegoat. This often led to isolation and sometimes mandatory time off. We can assure you: this mandatory time off is *not* a vacation. This time off is experienced as exile, both professionally and socially. Worse yet, in this "time off," the physician will often internalize this negative feedback and start to feel inferior, inadequate, guilty, and ashamed. If that individual is well-supported and can find a way to recognize their own humanity separate from their role as a physician, healing is possible. However, if they cannot overcome the intertwining of self and career, that individual is in danger of an existential crisis and significant mental health sequelae (Koretz, 2022). It is, perhaps, not hard to imagine why physician suicide is as high as it is.

Sometimes, we are asked, "So, why does anyone stay?" Certainly, there are pockets of healthcare where the leadership truly values the physician workforce and these physicians are thriving.

That is wonderful, when we see it. Some of the physicians we spoke with who are still practicing (while planning their escape), often cited reasons such as guilt, shame, fear, "golden handcuffs," and tactics by their leadership preying on these feelings. Sometimes a physician made it known that they were considering leaving. The physician was then shamed, and sometimes also offered a bonus to stay. These tactics are not corrective or conciliatory; they are coercive.

"It's like an abusive relationship. I tell them I'm leaving. They remind me that I'll never be anything on my own, and I'll wind up bankrupt if I leave. So, I stay, but the cycle continues."

Our colleagues told appalling stories of betrayal. Sometimes it was from inside their physician group or department. Sometimes it was at the institutional level. Many talked about how lawsuits and general lack of trust from society at large had been the underlying issue that ultimately culminated in the departure. Several spoke of being discredited as a means to be silenced, where leaving medicine was more being pushed or forced out.

The earliest version of this chapter was titled "gaslighting." This was because a significant percentage of our earliest interviewees had used this exact word and told incredibly similar stories of how things had gone badly, how they went to their administration, and how they were told that *they* were the problem and / or the problem was self-imagined. As the demographics of the research participant group grew more diverse, the manifestations of this "breach of trust" continued, while the phenomenon of gaslighting remained specific to female interviewees, especially if they were junior in rank. However, lack of honesty and breach of trust were critical components of nearly every story.

> *"I think doctors are more under the spotlight and, instead of being supportive of them, the medical organizations are putting them under the spotlight and are more apt to point fingers when things go badly."*

"You set me up to fail. You knew I was struggling at home. You knew I was struggling here. You knew I didn't have what I needed. You set me up. And I just didn't feel, I don't know ... I felt so defeated. I didn't feel like I could turn around and say that."

"I don't know who is for me. I don't know who I can trust."

"But, like, there are also the feelings of failure, and I'm not good enough. You know, why is everybody else fine with this, and I'm not fine with this? ... Maybe I'm just not tough enough."

The interviews were often very emotional. Consistently, tears and expletives cohabitated the space with stories of betrayal.

"They've totally just ground me into dust. And, you know, I've talked to them, you know, over the last several years about what needs to change for me to continue here. And they just don't care."

THE DOCTOR IS NO LONGER IN

"[I had] a lot of anger at the system, a lot of anger at patients. A lot of feelings of being a victim of this system and feeling invisible, that even when I felt like I was crying out for help, that my calls went unanswered."

"… it's all about the finances … when it's on the backs of the team … it's not care-centric. The doctors and nurses and nurse practitioners, they are the ones being humiliated. They are being minimized. That is a problem. 'Cause when we all leave, who is going to take care of these patients? That's what I'm concerned about."

"… it's the underlying things that are burning us out that they are not addressing. A lot of it is politics … But, more so, the way organizations say one thing and do another. 'Oh, we're very patient-centric.' Bullshit! Your actions don't show it."

"I feel like when I started medicine, I was a runner, and I was given a new pair of cleats and told to just go. I was, like, cool and after about five years, I feel like I was told I could still go, but these are hurdles, and we want you to jump. We want you to be a hurdler. I was like, alright, I can train, and I can become a hurdler. Then after about another five years, it was like, okay, now we're going to turn it into a steeplechase. We're going to add higher barriers, water features, and we're still gonna time you and want you to do it just as fast and just as accurately. Then at about year 20, I felt like someone tied a bungee cord around my waist, had a sumo wrestler holding on to each end of the cord and, like, okay now run. I'm just running in place .... I feel like there are just more and more things that are put into place for me to do as a physician that has nothing to do with medical care and care of patients."

Overall, a certain personality type self-selects into medicine. This person wants to excel and, often, academics is the primary mechanism for excellence (although, you will also find a number of perfectionists who are marathon runners, Olympic athletes, prima donnas, and concert pianists). These individuals often seek external validation. But there is an Achilles heel to this quality. This need for external validation makes one vulnerable to shame and has been recognized historically in medicine in that some of our most common teaching tactics prey on this phenomenon — "pimping," humiliating behavior in the OR, etc. A preceptor during medical school training once said, "There are two ways you learn in medicine: repetition and traumatic emotional experience [*i.e. humiliation*]." These behaviors have been woven throughout the culture of American academic medicine since its inception.

Because such an individual is prone to shame, the individual winds up internalizing the shame — and shame is a very dangerous emotion (Pronovost & Bienvenu, 2015; Brown, 2013; Brown, 2015). The dangers of shame are many; shame (1) increases the sense of vulnerability, and (2) in a very real way, increases the sense of vulnerability to the extent that "this situation has negatively affected my reputation" and "I am even more vulnerable now." This triggers a fight or flight response, and it manifests as needing an escape plan. It's not surprising that so many of our colleagues actually called it their "escape plan."

> ***"I feel like I am a mouse in a field and the hawks are circling."***

In her book *If I Betray These Words*, Wendy Dean highlights the stories of physicians who have suffered moral injury. One of the most striking is a story about a physician named Jay. By all accounts, Jay was a gregarious character and a fantastic physician. However, when he bumped up against his hospital administration due to his principles, he was labeled as "disruptive." It is a devastating story where he was then reported to the governing bodies, labeled with a mental health disorder, isolated, exiled, and shamed. He later died by suicide (Dean & Talbot, 2023).

During this project, we met another Ob/Gyn with a very similar story. She was a well-trained and energetic physician, liked by her team, and loved by patients. However, when leadership changed and policies were put in place that sacrificed patient safety, she spoke up. For a couple of years, it seemed like simple disagreements, but the administration had been collecting a folder of her "disruptive" behaviors. She was reported to the state board and forced to undergo anger-management classes. She was placed on probation. When she then displayed cynicism, she was again reported as "disruptive" and forced to enter a program or be fired. Because there were no other hospitals anywhere in the area and her son was in high school, to not follow instructions would be upsetting for her family. She did as she was told. She was then labeled with a mental health disorder and put on leave. During those dark days, she nearly died by suicide. With the help of friends and family, she is alive. After her son graduated high school, she moved to a new state, found a new position, and is currently "planning her escape" from clinical medicine.

Speaking out has very real consequences. So much so, that when the New York Times wanted to interview physicians on this subject last year, they couldn't find enough people to go on record. In the NYT, Eyal Press states:

> "Because doctors are highly skilled professionals who are not so easy to replace, I assumed that they would not be as reluctant to discuss the distressing conditions at their jobs as the low-wage workers I'd

interviewed. But the physicians I contacted were afraid to talk openly. 'I have since reconsidered this and do not feel this is something that I can do right now,' one doctor wrote to me. Another texted, 'will need to be anon.' Some sources I tried to reach had signed nondisclosure agreements that prohibited them from speaking with the media without permission. Others worried they could be disciplined or fired if they angered their employers" (Press, 2023).

Given these realities of shame and vulnerability in a system where adverse outcomes are inevitably going to occur, we need to discuss the bigger picture. We are now seeing that this same vulnerability to shame is being exploited when a healthcare system or entity needs to distance themselves from financial responsibility for something. This usually manifests as a bad patient outcome, which we know is really the product of systemic failure (Institute of Medicine (U.S.) Committee on Quality of Health Care in America, 2000). But, the physician becomes the scapegoat.

We heard from numerous physicians (especially from Radiology and Ob/Gyn) that a lawsuit had essentially ruined their life. Often, it wasn't the lawsuit itself, but how long it dragged on, how it impacted their reputation, and how it uncovered the lack of support and loyalty that they could expect from their home institutions. Basically, a lawsuit brought together the worst of the themes that we described into a concentrated situation: lack of control, lack of autonomy, feeling undervalued, feeling unappreciated, a sense of dehumanization, and breach of trust. In this case, the breach of trust was multiplied, because there was breach of trust between doctor and patient, between doctor and home institution, and between doctor and society. One such doctor reported feeling "abandoned" by everyone during his lawsuit, which lasted over seven years. That is a long time to sit with such a big emotion and still carry on with your day-to-day. It's not right to treat a human that way, especially when there was never any malice.

We have not met a physician that claims to have never made a mistake, and any physician that did would immediately be suspect. Because we all make mistakes. Doctors are humans, and humans make mistakes. However, there are two very frustrating things that stood out about the malpractice lawsuits reported by our interviewees: (1) the lawsuits were very often *not* for their actual mistakes, but for some other tangential and seemingly irrelevant aspect of the incident, and (2) medical malpractice lawsuits directly contradict patient safety teachings that medical errors most commonly occur because of systemic failures, and not the failing of one individual.

For example, one of our colleagues told us about her one malpractice suit. It wasn't due to a medical error, but a patient who sought a second opinion. Ultimately, the issue was about improper documentation, and it was settled out of court. The patient walked away with $100,000 because Epic (a major electronic health record system) was down when the patient was seen in the emergency room, and the handwritten notes of our colleague were unavailable to the treating physician. So the case was against "her", but really the error was a systematic error of a failed electronic health record system followed by improper administrative filing of the handwritten documentation.

However, the same individual admitted that she has made some pretty serious mistakes and was never sued for any of them. With her own hands, she had cut two ureters, caused several hemorrhages, and sent more than one person to the ICU unexpectedly. We would venture to guess that any honest pelvic surgeon would have similar reports. The point of this story is that none of those errors became a lawsuit. Very often, the mistakes and the lawsuits don't line up, and it is emotionally erosive for physicians to live in this vulnerable state of wondering when they will (often erroneously) be accused of something and suffer a miserable, lingering lawsuit that will haunt them for years.

We spoke with another doctor, also an Ob/gyn. She had delivered a baby that was known to have fetal anomalies, meaning that the pregnancy ultrasounds had already predicted that the newborn would have issues. The newborn did have issues and went on to have cognitive delay. The family was approached by a lawyer, and they sued.

Two and a half years later, the doctor ran into the family on the courthouse steps. They ran up to her, hugged her, and asked, "What are you doing here?"

"Of course, in my head, I wanted to shout, 'Are you kidding me?! You are suing me and ruining my life for something that I could not control!!'"

Not wanting to insult their intelligence and, ever the professional, she replied, ***"I have been named in this lawsuit you are bringing to the court today."***

"Oh no, we would never sue YOU. We love YOU. You took all that time explaining everything and showing us how to do the best for our daughter …"

This family sincerely did not understand the process. They just knew that their daughter had special needs, and a lawyer had approached them promising them the much-needed money to provide for those needs. This is an ethical mess. We need a system where this child gets what she needs, the family has the resources to provide for those needs, and this doctor does not have to live with an albatross around her neck for years for no reason.

The second major problem is that these lawsuits contradict the major tenets of patient safety. There is an entire science of patient safety. People like Peter Pronovost have written countless articles and books on this subject (Pronovost & Vohr, 2010; Laurance, 2009). Johns Hopkins has dedicated an entire institute to this science (*Armstrong Institute for Patient Safety and Quality*, n.d.). One of the first major teachings from any of these experts will tell you that nearly all medical errors are systematic. They are usually not a simple error by a single person. Therefore, when a medical error occurs, we will often perform what is called a Root Cause Analysis (RCA). These are very common in medicine. A common method is using the Swiss cheese model and seeing how the "holes" line up to allow a patient to slip through the cracks (Wiegmann et al., 2021). Another method is called the "fishbone" or the "5 whys" behind an error (Institute for Healthcare Improvement, 2019). To demonstrate these concepts, we will use a previous example: a transected ureter reported by one of our interviewees.

1. **Why did the ureter get transected?**

   Because there was unexpectedly dense cancer tissue surrounding the ureter at the level of the uterine artery

2. **Why was there unexpectedly dense cancer tissue?**

   Because the preoperative imaging did not suggest any such cancer in this location and the dissection was much too difficult for the surgical team available

3. Why did the preoperative imaging not suggest that this trouble was present?

Because there had been a 10-week delay between the imaging and surgery

4. Why was there a 10-week delay?

Because the patient's insurance company declined several peer-to-peer reviews prior to agreeing to pay for this procedure, but they would not cover repeat imaging given the delay this caused

5. Why was the dissection too difficult for the surgical team available?

Because there were no backup surgeons available for an unexpected finding such as this one and the OR team was not trained and dedicated for the specialty

6. Why was there a shortage of backup surgeons and a non-dedicated OR team?

Because this surgery was occurring "after hours" and into the night

7. Why was this surgery occurring "after hours" and into the night?

Because the primary surgeon did not have block time and therefore did not have a dedicated OR during regular business hours

8. Why did the primary surgeon not have block time?

Because there were competing demands within the hospital and the administration felt that there were inadequate resources to increase staffing and / or creation of more ORs

As you can see the *5 Whys* are often more than five, but you get the picture. When you do this kind of analysis, two things will become apparent. The problems almost always come down to having too little money and too little time. Another central concept is the breakdown of communication and failure of those involved to have a shared mental model of what is best for the ideal patient outcome. Having done this exercise, we see that it's not straightforward.

Not only does this leave physicians feeling like exposed mice in an open field with a hawk circling, but it's ominous for the future of patient safety. Study after study has shown that finger-pointing, blaming, and shaming are associated with *increased* errors in the future. So, the more that an institution, system, or society engages in this behavior, the more errors that will occur (Robertson & Long, 2019).

For those who have not yet been sued but see these issues all around them, they often become prone to what is colloquially called "CYA." CYA stands for "cover your ass." It is all too common for labs, imaging, consults, referrals, and even procedures to be done unnecessarily for "CYA" indications. The doctor knew that it was unlikely that the patient would have a terrible, rare condition, but ordered the MRI anyway. When asked why (informally, by another doctor), they will often admit that the indication for the imaging was "CYA." CYA partially explains the exceptionally high c-section rate in our country, and a host of other very invasive surgeries. Some refer to this as the practice of "defensive" medicine, pointing to the act of preemptively defending themselves from possible lawsuits. Not surprisingly, this continues the upward drive of healthcare costs.

The physicians we interviewed who were troubled by lawsuits generally didn't care about the money. Usually, it is going to be paid out by their malpractice insurance coverage through the hospital, anyway. It is the experience that is so gross. Doctors who experience lawsuits are more likely to experience depression, anxiety, addiction, divorce, and suicide (Vizcaíno-Rakosnik et al., 2020). All of these negative experiences erode trust. And, as is so key to this book, they are also much more likely to leave direct patient care.

To have a system that really serves all of us — as patients, as doctors, as hospital teams — there needs to be trust; there needs to be teamwork. Doctors need to be able to walk into the hospital without dread, without stopping in the parking garage and praying that no one will put them in a terrible situation today. Doctors need to walk into the hospital knowing that they are valued.

Part Three

The Path Ahead

"I had to not care about doing things in a high-quality way anymore just to get through the day. It's not OK. Things have to change."

— CARDIOLOGIST, 23 YEARS OF PRACTICE

THE DOCTOR IS NO LONGER IN

"What could keep me? An environment of trust, where it isn't designed to burn people out. It's designed around patients and around the people serving them. An environment with mutual respect ... where you support your physicians to care for patients and to teach, with dedicated time to think and to create. That's what I'm doing now. I'm exploring my options. I'm exploring what could be meaningful and impactful ... I need the freedom to create and build something that supports good patient care."

— INTERNAL MEDICINE HOSPITALIST,
22 YEARS OF PRACTICE

CHAPTER 8

Casualties
and Consequences

Through the stories shared in this book, we have gained insight into the experiences of today's U.S. physicians, thanks to the courage and candor of our interviewees. We have heard many tales of suffering. We have seen that some physicians can be healed, while others develop extreme symptoms, up to and including suicide. A significant risk factor that bore out separating these two groups was the individual's ability to separate their sense of self from their role as a physician.

If you are a physician and believe that is *all* that you are, losing or leaving your role as a physician creates an existential crisis. Similarly, when leadership mistreats physicians, we often internalize those critiques and toxic negative accusations, which is like drinking poison and has the same effect. To protect yourself, you must separate your humanity from your career and be extremely cautious about what is allowed to affect you at the core.

These observations were not reported directly from our interviewees. They are observations made by us as we heard the stories and saw which physicians had found their way out and were thriving and which ones were trapped in despair. These observations will require their own investigation in the future, but we believe they will play out in this process.

We have set up our healthcare system around money, and that is the foundation of the problems we face as healthcare professionals. It has led to a divisive erosion of trust. This sentiment was expressed by some of our participants in these ways:

"We learned about $5M worth of bonuses that the executives were giving themselves. The next week, I got an email that said, 'Despite the financial pressures … blah, blah, blah … we are going to give you a raise.' The raise was enough to buy me a couple cups of coffee a week. I mean, how am I supposed to take that? It's a slap in the face."

"A lot of medicine has become RVU-driven, including in academia. You need to see x number of patients, regardless of the amount of time you spend with them or the quality of care that you provide ... it's numbers, numbers, numbers."

"As part of my contract, I was promised the resources to open a clinic for management of addiction in this small town where there was nothing. After two years, I got another email that said, like ... "Blah, blah, given financial constraints, we can't ..." Two weeks later, I found out that the five people in the C-suite had given themselves bonuses totaling almost $12M at the end of the previous fiscal year. After that, I didn't last long."

Our colleagues who participated in this research project are not alone in recognizing greed in U.S. healthcare. Likely, you are able to pick up a newspaper right now and there is an article about it affecting a city near you. You are recognizing the problem. Those of us who follow medical literature have been reading about it increasingly over the past few years. In an article that makes us feel like we are not the only ones, Dr. Amanda Loudin is quoted saying, "Anyone who cares about patients is doomed to burnout" (Loudin, 2023). In *Harvard Magazine*, David Cutler notes that greed is one of the three major components of excessive health spending in the U.S.. You see this in the list price for medications, like insulin, that are up to 10 times higher than that in neighboring Canada. You see this in your hospital bill when a prestigious hospital charges multiple times what less prestigious hospitals do for the same service (Cutler, 2020).

In a beautifully crafted lecture, Don Berwick speaks to the dangers of greed in healthcare. He has since retired, but Don Berwick ran the Centers for Medicare and Medicaid for several decades. He now works with the Institute for Healthcare Improvement (IHI). In his keynote speech at the IHI Forum in 2022, he states,

> "The American healthcare industry is, I strongly suspect, today the largest machine for the regressive transfer of wealth from the poorer to the richer in the whole of our nation … Silence is a

sin" (Institute for Healthcare Improvement & Berwick, 2022).

We are so grateful that our colleagues did not remain silent. During our interviews, the themes that consistently emerged were lack of autonomy, burnout, dehumanization, moral injury, and breach of trust. Our colleagues leaving direct patient care told us they are feeling undervalued, minimized, patronized, insulted, morally compromised, and trapped without control. We processed what they told us and determined that these things are creating "the squeeze" on physicians that ultimately forces them out of direct patient care. One of our participants aptly described her experience with the notion of being in a box:

> ***"Like when you're underwater for such a long time, you think that's normal and then when all of a sudden you break the surface and you can, like, breathe fresh air. You can see the light not through water and not through filters, and it was, like, wow. I couldn't go back into that box again."***

Now, how do we integrate what we have learned from this research with the broader knowledge on the matter?

If we have learned nothing else from this experiment, we found that the problems are pervasive. These themes occurred all over the country in doctors who are all very different individuals practicing different specialties in different settings. There are universal and fundamental flaws in our healthcare system, and they are driving physicians away from direct patient care.

Sometimes, public health experts and clinical researchers talk about "person-years." When we want to see how much humanity is affected by a disease, we think not just about the number of deaths, but how many years of life were lost with each death. If a person was 90 at the time of death, the years of life lost are few. If, however, a person dies at age 20, that was another 70 years of life lost. How many doctor-years are being lost in this exodus? This chapter is dedicated to questions like this one. Questions that address the downstream effects of what is occurring today.

Many physicians enter the field driven by a deep desire to help others, alleviate suffering, and contribute to improved health outcomes. This intrinsic motivation fuels their dedication and resilience. Building trust and rapport with patients, witnessing their healing journeys, and making a tangible difference in their lives are deeply rewarding aspects of being a physician. The enduring calling of physicians to care for patients is clashing with the unsustainable realities of practicing medicine in the current U.S. healthcare environment. Addressing this challenge requires acknowledging both sides: appreciating the unwavering calling of physicians while recognizing the need for systemic changes to make their practice more sustainable.

Many of the physicians that we interviewed who left said that they needed a period of recovery. But after the recovery, most everyone planned on using their education, skills, and training to try to make things better — to continue to serve humanity. Careers we were told about include: health policy, writing, teaching, clinical research, pharmaceutical industry, working for the FDA / CDC / WHO, and entrepreneurship around health. One surgeon even applied for citizenship to the European Union to continue to practice in a different healthcare environment. These are people who did not start practicing with the intent to leave. They just felt that the environment was not conducive to the way that they wanted to practice medicine and were essentially pushed into the momentous decision to exit clinical practice.

As these physicians move on to their new roles, recruitment of physicians from other countries to the U.S. increases. This exacerbates the "brain drain" globally (Ebeye & Lee, 2023). Interestingly, it does allow some increased diversity to be brought back into the care of U.S. patients, but perhaps this also leaves the patients of the U.S. with fewer doctors who match their own demographics. These phenomena threaten to erode the already limited progress we have made in diversifying the U.S. healthcare workforce, which we know is critical to optimal outcomes. The physicians who are leaving are more likely to be female and represent individuals with variations of lived experience and of demographics that represent historically marginalized groups. This hinders our ability to provide culturally competent care. It negatively impacts physician-patient relationships, and it worsens healthcare outcomes. The gaps will continue to widen.

As we have fewer doctors to care for everyone, we will all feel it. But some patients will feel the effects much worse than others. We are already seeing exacerbated inequities in particularly impoverished Black communities that will continue to worsen, and we can expect similar trends in other marginalized communities. One of the most glaring examples where we can already see the effects of this crisis are in the Black maternal mortality rates. It was always appalling, but the gap between the death rates of white moms and Black moms has doubled over the last 30 years because marginalized populations are affected first. The communities where Black women are giving birth have had many of their hospitals closed already. Their obstetric care is disjointed, under-resourced, and prone to error — even more than the baseline. This is all outlined in a brilliant documentary titled, *Aftershock* (Eiselt & Lewis Lee, 2022).

We also spoke with physicians who have started or joined concierge practice or direct-care models. Concierge medicine works differently than what U.S. citizens are used to seeing. These models take insurance out of the equation, so that a patient pays an annual fee to a doctor who has a small number of patients. In exchange, this doctor is now available when they are needed by any patient in their practice. It was once only for the wealthy. Now, it's for people with a little extra cash who are just frustrated that they can't get in to see their doctor and are tired of the struggle. These people usually do end up keeping their insurance as well, which will still cover labs, imaging, etc., as well or as poorly as before. But at least their doctor answers the phone.

Some doctors have made this choice in lieu of completely leaving medicine, or other more drastic measures. They felt that it was the only way that they could continue to practice medicine properly.

"My choices were to either provide quality care to some or inadequate care to many," was the reasoning of one such physician. This reasoning demonstrates how far we can be forced to stray from what many physicians consider to be an ideal of medicine, which is to provide care for individuals regardless of ability to pay.

Perhaps the most concerning and dire consequence of the physician exodus is the vital role doctors play in the, albeit broken, healthcare system. While the current system has many weak links that contribute to its failing, the growing deficit of doctors will no doubt accelerate the looming disaster of this system's collapse.

LOGIC EXERCISE

Assumption 1: Physicians are a core resource of our healthcare system.

Assumption 2: The healthcare system is employing behaviors that are consistently driving physicians away.

Assumption 3: Any society or organization that routinely sacrifices its core resources will ultimately collapse.

Result: Our healthcare system will collapse.

We are hoping that Assumption 1 is generally accepted, and we believe that it is. We are also hoping that in this book, we have convinced you that Assumption 2 is correct. Assumption 3 is supported by Jared Diamond in his book *Collapse: How Societies Decide to Fail or Succeed*. In this book, he tells stories of societies that made critical decisions in both positive and negative directions. He finds the commonalities of these decisions throughout history and then applies them to today's world. In this text, Diamond states, "a system that sacrifices its most important resources for short-term gain will collapse" (Diamond,

2011). If this is true, and we believe that it is, the U.S. healthcare system is on a trajectory for collapse. We are not the first to suggest this scenario. Other well-respected physicians and experts have also made this statement (Glatter, Papadakos, & Shah, 2023).

CHAPTER 9

Where Are We Headed?

"Ingenuity is often misunderstood. It is not a matter of superior intelligence, but of character. It demands, more than anything, a willingness to recognize failure. To not paper over the cracks and to change. It arises from deliberate, even obsessive, reflection on failure and a constant searching for new solutions." (Gawande, 2014)

— ATUL GAWANDE, SURGEON, WRITER, PUBLIC HEALTH RESEARCHER

We cannot support a system that allows capitalization on the suffering of others. We have no love for this broken system. But we have much love for the people trapped inside of it. If you are one of those individuals, there are some things we want you to know:

1) You are not alone. This book was written because we felt like you. We met hundreds of colleagues with shared experiences in the making of this book. Then we heard from over a thousand more as we started doing interviews to promote the book. We know that you are very likely being told that the problem is you. It is not you. *You are not the problem.*

2) Although you are not the problem, this could become a very dangerous problem *for* you. Some of our colleagues found healing. Some lost their lives to suicide. Most are stuck in between these extremes. There are established protective factors, such as a supportive spouse, strong social networks, etc. You inherently know this, and you are capable enough to read about healthy coping mechanisms and wellness. But the one new thing that we can offer is our observation about who healed and who didn't.

Those who healed were able to recognize that they are a human first. They know that being a doctor, while a very important part of their identity, is not their entire identity. In addition, they honored and protected this recognition of their own humanity and treated themselves with respect, even when their leadership did not. You can listen to critiques, but if you are being fed toxic information about yourself and you sense that it is not being delivered by someone who has your best interests at heart, do not drink that poison. Do not internalize all of the negative messages you are being fed. If you must sift through a collection of negative messages, do it with help from those who love and support you. You will need help assessing what information might be valuable and what needs to be set aside before it is consumed and festers in your soul.

Wherever possible, also discuss this information with someone who is removed from the entire story (a therapist or old friend with no direct connection). Your friends from work will likely have difficulty remaining objective. Similarly, your partner is also likely stressed by this situation and may have difficulty remaining objective. We spoke with several individuals who felt trapped in their careers, but were married to spouses who feared how a career change would impact the family and finances. Understandably, this compounds the weight of such conversations. Objectivity allows a fresh perspective.

We need healing. We need our physicians to thrive. The next phases for our healthcare system are going to be complex and will require recognition that everyone within is human, deserves respect, and has a role in creating a system that serves us all. Although we foresee a collapse, overhaul, and rebuilding, we want to protect the human individuals currently within this system. When we rebuild, physicians will need to come to the table and work as a team with other stakeholders. With these stakeholders, we will need to cease zero sum thinking and instead work as a team. We are all going to win or lose together.

There are very few people benefiting from the current system. Patients are not benefiting, nor are physicians. One of our participants aptly stated,

"Nobody's actually coming to save this thing ... someone's winning in the current system, and it's not us, and it's not patients, and I'm not sure I can fix it by myself."

Everybody else on the healthcare team is struggling, too. Even hospital administrators are finding themselves in difficult positions. They can't control the amount of money coming in and have little control over reimbursement models. Certainly, the U.S. taxpayers are not benefiting, and a tremendous amount of money is being wasted.

It would seem the only individuals still benefiting are high-level executives in healthcare systems (many now owned by private equity), insurance companies and pharmaceutical / industry companies. There is also a strong tide of indifference in upper-level institutional management at many hospitals and medical institutions. Human behavior tends toward inertia. If a system is working for you, you will not be inclined to change it. The few who are benefiting and / or are indifferent are in positions of power, and that makes change difficult.

ROAD MAP FOR SYSTEMIC CHANGE

In preparation for this book, we amassed information from our interviews against the backdrop of current literature and expert thought about our healthcare system. In addition to interviewing physicians, which was the main goal of the book, we also spoke with many other stakeholders: lay people, patients, nurses, hospital administrators, business executives, etc. It seems that the best way for things to start is with our insurance companies and how we structure health plans.

Insurance companies will need to acknowledge some difficult truths: (1) their business model was designed with a fundamental flaw, (2) the business model that is currently U.S. health insurance is a dinosaur that is no longer serving its purpose, and (3) when businesses are dinosaurs, they must adapt or die. In his book *Ripple of Change*, Dr. Todd Otten reviews data on the number of roles between the doctor and patient and how that number has changed over time (Otten & Judy, 2023). Over the past 50 years, the average number went from one to 17. Seventeen! Seventeen people between the doctor and the patient getting what she needs. No wonder our system feels so bloated and ineffective. We foresee that some savvy health insurance executives will recognize these phenomena and realize that the 17 people between doctor and patient are largely their employees. We need to remove those employees from the current, obstructive roles into supportive roles. In doing so, they will change the structure of their own business model.

We need to change the way we think about the problem, and therefore the solutions. If we put the patient at the center of the model, rather than money, we can imagine ways to design a system around what we would like to see for patients. Once we can establish those things, then (and only then) should we design reimbursement structures. Our proposal that change will have to start with the insurance companies and the structuring of health plans is also supported by Michael Porter, a world-renowned economist:

> "The legacy of many health plans is a culture of denial: denial of claims, denial of services, denial of choice, denial of physician autonomy, and denial of responsibility for members' health results. While health plans are trying to move away from this culture, most retain the paternalistic view that they need to oversee provider processes with pay for performance and to continue to constrain members' choice of providers via networks. Health plans must replace the culture of denial with a culture of patient health ... Responsiveness, fairness, consistency, reliability, integrity, and the ability to listen will be needed in

every interaction with every party to dismantle the distrust that has accumulated. Those health plans that succeed in moving in the directions we have outlined will have employees who are far more motivated and dedicated ... The satisfaction of creating value for patients and working with providers centered on results instead of restricting and second-guessing decisions will be palpable for all concerned" (Porter & Teisberg, 2006).

Unfortunately, we don't have a blank slate on which to design a new model. Instead, we have an increasingly complex system that keeps trying to course correct. With each correction, we have added administrative roles that are essentially functioning in between the doctor and the patient. All of those prior authorization forms and peer-to-peer conversations, justifications with insurance companies, billing management, coding management, documentation correction, etc., are now real jobs for real people. Real people need real jobs that put real food on the table. Any plans to make these much needed changes will have to thoughtfully consider how the above-mentioned roles can be shifted. Some of the individuals we spoke with described it as having "gone to the dark side," but most simply felt that the needs of their families superseded amorphous altruism. They all reported that they now had what they needed to thrive: reasonable schedules, autonomy, work-life balance, and job stability.

What if we did start shifting those roles a bit? What if the nurse that is reading prior authorization forms instead does patient education over the phone? What about the physician employed by the insurance company that needs convincing in the peer-to-peer? That person has a wealth of knowledge. What if that person became a remote provider for those few patients with extraordinarily complex situations who need a doctor that functions as a consultant and continues to work remotely? We are suggesting that we remove the roles that obstruct care between the doctor and patient, create roles that instead support that care, and find innovative ways to employ many of these same individuals so that very few people are left unemployed and most can keep the job qualities that drew them to that position in the first place: reasonable schedules, autonomy, work-life balance, and job stability.

But we also need to cut back on spending. We have decided 18% of our GDP is too much to spend. That will occur when we catch and treat the cancer early, control the diabetes, and avoid the expensive surgery, etc. This comes with improved outcomes and less waste. Accountable Care Organizations (ACO) were designed for this reason and are being created across the country. Essentially, they flip the reimbursement model. Instead of reimbursing on a fee-for-service basis, they provide a large sum of money to a hospital system to keep a large group of people well. ACOs can be very successful and, if run properly, can save a lot of money. The saved money is usually called "shared savings." One of the major reasons that ACOs have not caught on is because that "shared savings" is supposed to be put back into the system that saved the money — more staff, better clinics, more community health initiatives, bonuses for team players, etc. Instead, that money is often siphoned off and given away to shareholders and other interested parties who were not part of the ACO's success. This deflates the whole system. Morale cannot be maintained, if the fruits of the team's labor are routinely squandered or stolen.

Wendy Dean tells such a story in her book, *If I Betray These Words*. She tells the story of a doctor named Stuart who created an ACO and provided great primary care. When the shared savings were realized, "it went straight to [the hospital's] central business office. As it trickled down through the layers of the organization on its way to Stuart's team … each layer took a cut. By the time it got to Stuart and his team, it was a sliver of the millions his team had earned, and it wasn't enough to support more staff" (Dean & Talbot, 2023). Although no laws were broken in this story, it sounds like stealing. And it likely feels that way to those who worked so hard for those "shared savings" under the guise that the shared savings would be used to increase staff and further improve what they were building. Given stories such as this, it's not surprising that ACOs haven't gained momentum. But ideas such as these have real potential.

These are not new suggestions. Nearly two decades ago, Michael Porter also proposed:

> *"Imagine if a health plan were seen as an expert on health and the member's greatest advocate?"*
>
> *"Imagine if the health plan informed and advised members and reduced the anxiety of illness?"*
>
> *"Imagine if members knew that their health plan was dedicated to getting the best provider for their condition?"*

THE DOCTOR IS NO LONGER IN

"If health plans were truly dedicated to health, the consequences in terms of creativity, innovation, and health care value would be enormous."

(Healthcare) Competition takes place on discrete interventions, rather than the full cycle of care, where value is determined. Value can only be measured over the care cycle — not for an individual procedure, service, office visit or test.

He also says:

Competition has gravitated to a zero sum competition, in which the gains of one system participant come at the expense of others ... Zero sum competition is not inherent in the nature of competition.

And finally:

The many talented and well-intended individuals working in the system are often working at cross purposes to patient value. They are increasingly aware of, and disheartened by, this conflict ... The only real solution is to unite all participants in the system for a common purpose.

We concur. (If you want to read a thorough and thoughtful dissertation on the matter from a true economic genius, please see "Redefining Health Care") (Porter & Teisberg, 2006).

And what did we learn about lawsuits and defensive medicine? Tort reform will save the U.S. a significant amount of money, numerous physicians, unwanted gross feelings, and future medical errors. We have been lobbying for this for decades, and it's going to cost us too many lives. Anything that is consistently driving doctors away from direct patient care needs to be halted.

Finally, we want to bring it back to the physicians, who are ultimately the focus of this book. We need to change the way physicians are valued by their institutions and employers. This requires putting down on paper what the traits, experiences, skills, and passions that each individual brings to the table, and importantly, how we can include that into how they are compensated and in their career development. How can we look beyond their role as a cog providing the commodity of medicine where the only value we can identify is the ability to make money for this broken system? We need to think creatively and find ways to concretely implement the statement of Dr. Carrie Cunningham, mentioned earlier in this book:

THE DOCTOR IS NO LONGER IN

> *"Physicians need to practice in a space where this is a cultural norm."*
>
> *We want you here.*
>
> *We value you.*
>
> *Your feelings are valid.*

Physicians need to know this from their institutions as "I trust that you value me as a person, you value what I have to offer the team, and you value my words. You will support me. You will provide what is needed to care for my patients. If / when something happens that we didn't want to happen, you will support me, and you won't silence me. You won't label me as a bad doctor. You won't discredit me. You won't sacrifice my career to distance the facility from the outcome."

> *"I think the toxicity is something that needs to be changed. We need to counter it with loving people and with perspective."*

The answer will require valuing everyone involved and building trust. The reimbursement model will be developed secondarily to support quality outcomes and value-based care. How this will be implemented depends on the stakeholders and who is willing to be at the forefront of revolutionizing, revitalizing, and innovating our system. Will it be the insurance companies or the CEOs of large hospital systems? Or will it be the growing platforms from programs such as CVSHealth?

Regardless of who makes the first move, when this happens, we can lay the foundation for shifts toward healthcare instead of illness care, and health insurance instead of illness insurance. People can start having more control over their own health. The focus can shift toward the fundamentals of health: clean air, clean water, healthy food, active lifestyles, and preventive maintenance. As much as possible, preventive maintenance will be provided in the community, close to peoples' homes so that no one has to find transportation to a major hospital just to get basic preventative care. Hospitals should be for advanced care. When your local community physician has identified a need for a specialist, then you will be sent to the large hospital. In this way, everyone on the team is working to the top of their ability, finds joy in their work, and is valued as a human being.

In the creation of this imagined system, the experts have displayed consilience and ingenuity. In Don Berwick's address to the IHI Forum (2022), where he admonishes the role of greed in our current healthcare system, he calls for "making noise" to help bring about change. Our stories shared in this book contribute depth and dimension — "make noise" — to the crisis faced by physicians (Institute for Healthcare Improvement & Berwick, 2022).

We are so grateful for the efforts of the experts listed above. We saw these same characteristics in our courageous colleagues who shared their stories to allow for the writing of this book. Ultimately, everyone quoted displayed this courage of character. We hope that their efforts will be honored with a response showing the courage to accept the need for a new environment in U.S. healthcare. We must allow the physicians to do what they do best — in an environment where they feel valued, supported, and unencumbered.

We have been talking about change for many years, but now people are starting to demand change. Momentum is gathering across all stakeholder groups — from patient advocates to physician groups to national organizations. Each person has a role to play in the transformation of our healthcare system, because we are all ultimately affected by it. Health is vital to our sense of self, our ability to engage in our lives, and how our society thrives.

American architect and inventor Buckminster Fuller said, "You never change things by fighting the existing reality. To change something, build a new model that makes the existing model obsolete."

The time is now. Together, let us build a new model.

NOTES

AUTHORS' NOTES

1. Koretz, J. (2022, November 17). What happens when your career becomes your whole identity. Harvard Business Review. https://hbr.org/2019/12/what-happens-when-your-career-becomes-your-whole-identity
2. Charmaz, K (2014). Constructing Grounded Theory: Second Edition, Sage Publications.

PART ONE

Chapter 1

1. Owen, L. L. W., Chang, T. H., & Manning, J. R. (2021). High-level cognition during story listening is reflected in high-order dynamic correlations in neural activity patterns. Nature Communications, 12(1). https://doi.org/10.1038/s41467-021-25876-x
2. Academic Surgical Congress, & Cunningham, C. (2023, March 3). 2023 AAS Presidential Address- Removing the mask [Video]. YouTube. https://www.youtube.com/watch?v=JaNBH4UPHv4

Chapter 2

1. Darves, B. (2014, July 23). Understanding the physician employment "Movement." NEJM CareerCenter. https://resources.nejmcareercenter.org/article/understanding-the-physician-employment-movement/
2. American Medical Association. (2023, July 12). AMA examines a decade of change in physician practice ownership and organization. https://www.ama-assn.org/press-center/press-releases/ama-examines-decade-change-physician-practice-ownership-and

3. Papanicolas, I., Woskie, L. R., & Jha, A. K. (2018). Health care spending in the United States and other High-Income countries. JAMA, 319(10), 1024. https://doi.org/10.1001/jama.2018.1150
4. Gunja, M., Gumas, E., Masitha, R., & Zephyrin, L. (2024). Insights into the U.S. Maternal Mortality Crisis: An International Comparison. The Commonwealth Fund. https://doi.org/10.26099/cthn-st75
5. Rothenberger, D. A. (2017). Physician Burnout and Well-Being: A Systematic Review and Framework for Action. Diseases of the Colon & Rectum, 60(6), 567–576. https://doi.org/10.1097/dcr.0000000000000844
6. Abbasi, J. (2022). Pushed to their limits, 1 in 5 physicians intends to leave practice. JAMA, 327(15), 1435. https://doi.org/10.1001/jama.2022.5074
7. American Medical Association, & Berg, S. (2023, November 28). 40% of doctors eye exits. What can organizations do to keep them? American Medical Association. https://www.ama-assn.org/practice-management/sustainability/40-doctors-eye-exits-what-can-organizations-do-keep-them
8. Shanafelt, T. D., Dyrbye, L. N., West, C. P., Sinsky, C., Tutty, M., Carlasare, L. E., Wang, H., & Trockel, M. (2021). Suicidal ideation and attitudes regarding help seeking in U.S. physicians relative to the U.S. working population. Mayo Clinic Proceedings, 96(8), 2067–2080. https://doi.org/10.1016/j.mayocp.2021.01.033
9. Glatter R, Papadakos P, Shah Y. The Coming Collapse of the U.S. Healthcare System. TIME, January 2023. https://time.com/6246045/collapse-us-health-care-system/
10. Jiang, J. X., Krishnan, R., & Bai, G. (2023). Price Transparency in Hospitals—Current research and future directions. JAMA Network Open, 6(1), e2249588. https://doi.org/10.1001/jamanetworkopen.2022.49588

11. Gottlieb S. (2000). Medical bills account for 40% of bankruptcies. BMJ (Clinical research ed.), 320(7245), 1295. https://www.ncbi.nlm.nih.gov/pmc/articles/PMC1127305/
12. Himmelstein, D. U., Lawless, R. M., Thorne, D., Foohey, P., & Woolhandler, S. (2019). Medical bankruptcy: still common despite the Affordable Care Act. American Journal of Public Health, 109(3), 431–433. https://doi.org/10.2105/ajph.2018.304901
13. Makary M. (2012). Unaccountable: What Hospitals Won't Tell You and How Transparency can Revolutionize Health Care, Bloomsbury Press.

PART TWO

"The Squeeze"

1. Charmaz, K. (2014). Constructing grounded theory. SAGE Publications Limited.
2. Shanafelt, T. D., Bradley, K. A., Wipf, J. E., & Back, A. L. (2002). Burnout and Self-Reported Patient care in an internal medicine residency program. Annals of Internal Medicine, 136(5), 358. https://doi.org/10.7326/0003-4819-136-5-200203050-00008
3. Maslach, C., & Leiter, M. P. (2016). Understanding the burnout experience: recent research and its implications for psychiatry. World Psychiatry, 15(2), 103–111. https://doi.org/10.1002/wps.20311
4. Dean, W., & Talbot, S. (2023). If I betray these words: Moral Injury in Medicine and Why It's So Hard for Clinicians to Put Patients First. Steerforth.

Chapter 3

1. Otten, T. R., & Judy, J. J. (2023). Ripple of change.
2. Vogel, S. Healthcare worker exodus continued through 2022. Definitive Healthcare. https://www.healthcaredive.com/news/healthcare-worker-exodus-physician-burnout-definitive/696769/

Chapter 4
1. Maslach, C., & Leiter, M. P. (2016). Understanding the burnout experience: recent research and its implications for psychiatry. World Psychiatry, 15(2), 103–111. https://doi.org/10.1002/wps.20311
2. Shanafelt TD, Bradley KA, Wipf JE, Back AL. Burnout and self-reported patient care in an internal medicine residency program. Ann Intern Med. 2002;136:358-67.
3. Dr. Tait Shanafelt has many publications on burnout. This meta-analysis article by Emma Yasinski is also thorough and poignant. https://ashpublications.org/ashclinicalnews/news/4167/Rethinking-Burnout
4. World Health Organization: WHO. (2019, May 28). Burn-out an "occupational phenomenon": International Classification of Diseases. World Health Organization. https://www.who.int/news/item/28-05-2019-burn-out-an-occupational-phenomenon-international-classification-of-diseases

Chapter 5
1. Academic Surgical Congress, & Cunningham, C. (2023, March 3). 2023 AAS Presidential Address- Removing the mask [Video]. YouTube. https://www.youtube.com/watch?v=JaNBH4UPHv4
2. Adebayo, N. A., Madorsky, T. Z., Alhalel, J., Post, S. L., O'Brian, C. A., & Simon, M. A. (2021). Underrepresented Minority (URM) physician exploitation exacerbated by the COVID-19 pandemic: Implications to URM physician-faculty burnout and worsening health disparities. Harvard public health review (Cambridge, Mass.), 30, https://hphr.org/30-article-adebayo/.
3. Paturel, A. (2022, June 29). Why women leave medicine. AAMC. https://www.aamc.org/news/why-women-leave-medicine
4. Frank, E., Zhao, Z., Sen, S., & Guille, C. (2019). Gender disparities in work and parental status among early career physicians. JAMA Network Open, 2(8), e198340. https://doi.org/10.1001/jamanetworkopen.2019.8340

5. Ligibel, J. A., Goularte, N., Berliner, J. I., Bird, S. B., Brazeau, C. M. L. R., Rowe, S. G., Stewart, M. T., & Trockel, M. T. (2023). Well-Being parameters and intention to leave current institution among academic physicians. JAMA Network Open, 6(12), e2347894. https://doi.org/10.1001/jamanetworkopen.2023.47894
6. Silver, J. K., Bean, A. C., Slocum, C., Poorman, J. A., Tenforde, A., Blauwet, C. A., Kirch, R. A., Parekh, R., Amonoo, H. L., Zafonte, R., & Osterbur, D. (2019). Physician Workforce Disparities and Patient Care: A Narrative review. Health Equity, 3(1), 360–377. https://doi.org/10.1089/heq.2019.0040

Chapter 6

1. Dean, W., Talbot, S. G., & Caplan, A. (2020). Clarifying the language of clinician distress. JAMA, 323(10), 923. https://doi.org/10.1001/jama.2019.21576
2. Dean, W., & Talbot, S. (2023). If I betray these words: Moral Injury in Medicine and Why It's So Hard for Clinicians to Put Patients First. Steerforth.
3. Makary M. (2012). Unaccountable: What Hospitals Won't Tell You and How Transparency can Revolutionize Health Care, Bloomsbury Press.
4. Dimick, J. B., Weeks, W. B., Karia, R. J., Das, S., & Campbell, D. A. (2006). Who pays for poor surgical quality? Building a business case for quality improvement. Journal of the American College of Surgeons, 202(6), 933–937. https://doi.org/10.1016/j.jamcollsurg.2006.02.015
5. Clifton, G. (2008). Flatlined: Resuscitating American Medicine, Rutgers University Press.

Chapter 7

1. Bowers, B. (2023, December 1). Bryce Bowers, DO. SoMeDocs: Doctors on Social Media. https://doctorsonsocialmedia.com/bryce-bowers-do/

2. Koretz, J. (2022, November 17). What happens when your career becomes your whole identity. Harvard Business Review. https://hbr.org/2019/12/what-happens-when-your-career-becomes-your-whole-identity
3. Pronovost, P. J., & Bienvenu, O. J. (2015). From shame to guilt to love. JAMA, 314(23), 2507. https://doi.org/10.1001/jama.2015.11521
4. Brown, B. (2013, January 15). Shame vs. guilt. Brené Brown. https://brenebrown.com//articles//2013//01//15//shame-v-guilt//
5. Brown, B. (2015). Daring greatly: How the Courage to Be Vulnerable Transforms the Way We Live, Love, Parent, and Lead. Penguin.
6. Dean, W., & Talbot, S. (2023). If I betray these words: Moral Injury in Medicine and Why It's So Hard for Clinicians to Put Patients First. Steerforth.
7. Press, E. (2023, July 14). The moral crisis of America's doctors: The corporatization of health care has changed the practice of medicine, causing many physicians to feel alienated from their work. The New York Times. https://www.nytimes.com/2023/06/15/magazine/doctors-moral-crises.html
8. Institute of Medicine (U.S.) Committee on Quality of Health Care in America, Kohn, L. T., Corrigan, J. M., & Donaldson, M. S. (Eds.). (2000). To Err is Human: Building a Safer Health System. National Academies Press (U.S.).
9. Pronovost, P. J., & Vohr, E. (2010). Safe patients, smart hospitals: How One Doctor's Checklist Can Help Us Change Health Care from the Inside Out. Penguin.
10. Laurance, J. (2009). Peter Pronovost: champion of checklists in critical care. Lancet, 374(9688), 443. https://doi.org/10.1016/s0140-6736(09)61439-2
11. Armstrong Institute for Patient Safety and Quality. (n.d.). Johns Hopkins Medicine. https://www.hopkinsmedicine.org//armstrong-institute

12. Wiegmann, D. A., Wood, L. J., Cohen, T. N., & Shappell, S. A. (2021). Understanding the "Swiss cheese model" and its application to patient safety. Journal of Patient Safety, 18(2), 119–123. https://doi.org/10.1097/pts.0000000000000810
13. Institute for Healthcare Improvement. (2019). Patient Safety Essentials Toolkit: 5 Whys: Finding the root cause of a problem. In Patient Safety Essentials Toolkit. https://www.ihi.org/sites/default/files/SafetyToolkit_5Whys.pdf
14. Robertson, J. J., & Long, B. (2019). Medicine's shame problem. Journal of Emergency Medicine, 57(3), 329–338. https://doi.org/10.1016/j.jemermed.2019.06.034
15. Vizcaíno-Rakosnik, M., Martin-Fumadó, C., Arimany-Manso, J., & Gómez-Durán, E. L. (2020). The impact of Malpractice Claims on Physicians' Well-Being and Practice. Journal of Patient Safety, 18(1), 46–51. https://doi.org/10.1097/pts.0000000000000800
16. Gawande A. (2104). Being Mortal: Medicine and What Matters in the End, Metropolitan Books.

PART THREE

Chapter 8

1. Loudin, A. (2023, February 24). "Only a sociopath could work for a large health system," Doc says sardonically. Medscape. https://www.medscape.com//viewarticle//988422?form=fpf
2. Cutler, D. The World's Costliest Health Care. Harvard Magazine, May-June 2020. https://www.harvardmagazine.com/2020/04/feature-forum-costliest-health-care
3. Institute for Healthcare Improvement, & Berwick, D. (2022, December 16). Salve lucrum – IHI Forum 2022 Keynote Address – Don Berwick [Video]. YouTube. https://www.youtube.com/watch?v=eErdxYZ7BSM

4. Ebeye, T., & Lee, H. (2023). Down the brain drain: a rapid review exploring physician emigration from West Africa. Global Health Research and Policy, 8(1). https://doi.org/10.1186/s41256-023-00307-0

5. Eiselt, P., & Lewis Lee, T. (Directors). (2022, January 23). Aftershock (F. De Souza & S. Prasad, Eds.). Impact Partners., Malka Films., Good Gravy Films., JustFilms/Ford Foundation. https://www.aftershockdocumentary.com/

6. Diamond, J. (2011). Collapse: How Societies Choose to Fail or Succeed: Revised Edition. Penguin.

7. Glatter R, Papadakos P, Shah Y. The Coming Collapse of the U.S. Healthcare System. TIME, January 2023. https://time.com/6246045/collapse-us-health-care-system/

Chapter 9

1. Gawande A. Being Mortal: Medicine and What Matters in the End, Metropolitan Books, 2014.Otten, T. R., & Judy, J. J. (2023). Ripple of change.

2. Porter, M. E., & Teisberg, E. O. (2006). Redefining health care: Creating Value-based Competition on Results. Harvard Business Press.

3. Dean, W., & Talbot, S. (2023). If I betray these words: Moral Injury in Medicine and Why It's So Hard for Clinicians to Put Patients First. Steerforth.

4. Academic Surgical Congress, & Cunningham, C. (2023, March 3). 2023 AAS Presidential Address- Removing the mask [Video]. YouTube. https://www.youtube.com/watch?v=JaNBH4UPHv4

5. Institute for Healthcare Improvement, & Berwick, D. (2022, December 16). Salve lucrum – IHI Forum 2022 Keynote Address – Don Berwick [Video]. YouTube. https://www.youtube.com/watch?v=eErdxYZ7BSM

ACKNOWLEDGEMENTS

As with anything worth doing, the creation of this book required a significant amount of effort. We could never have done it alone. First, we need to thank Dr. Ana Paula Cupertino for insisting that these two busy surgeon mothers meet over coffee. It took months of her pushing us into that blind date! We need to thank Dr. Timothy Dye for connecting us with our publisher (who didn't work out, but we are very grateful nonetheless). The fact that a major publisher picked it up so quickly gave us the confidence and legitimacy we needed in the early phases of this work.

Next, we are grateful to our team of research assistants, including Julia Schlossman, Nicky Wu, Alexandra Morrell, Natalie Wolfeiler, and Sunny Zhang. Thank you to the many, many individuals who helped edit and review the manuscript: Wendy Dean, Todd Otten, Gabe Charbonneau, Lisa Scardina, Jodie Green, John Smith, Doreen Bolhuis, Holly Dunn, Andrea Merrill, Jim Nathan, Diane Saunders, Morgan Mandigo, Kari Hastings, Vickie Swisher, and Debbie Frank.

THE DOCTOR IS NO LONGER IN

There are, no doubt, people forgotten from this list, and we apologize for any oversight. We are grateful to everyone for the tremendous support required to see this project to completion.

www.ingramcontent.com/pod-product-compliance
Lightning Source LLC
Chambersburg PA
CBHW052129030426
42337CB00028B/5090